"Randy Newman has done it again! His latest book on personal evangelism is so captivating and inspirational that I read it in one sitting."
—**Dr. Lyle Dorsett**, Billy Graham Professor of Evangelism at
Beeson Divinity School, Samford University

"This book left me confident in God's creative ability to reach into difficult souls and woo them to the Savior. The stories of how real people encounter Jesus remind us that God's work is a symphony. Different movements in the music move different people at opportune times. Newman's instructive comments amount to an 'on the job' apprenticeship in evangelism. God continues to work in even the most unlikely places."
—**Gregory E. Ganssle**, professor of philosophy at Talbot School
of Theology and author of *Our Deepest Desires*

"Looking for an infusion of hope and faith? Read Randy Newman's *Unlikely Converts* and you will be joyfully surprised. First that those you'd least expect can come to saving faith in Jesus Christ, and second that God can use your prayers, life, and words to make the gospel known. Full of amazing stories of God's pursuit of the lost and practical real-life application, Newman's warmth, humor, and storytelling make this an enjoyable and powerful read that you'll want to share with others."
—**Dr. Joel S. Woodruff**, president of The C. S. Lewis Institute

"In the course of my ministry, I have benefited enormously from Randy Newman's insights into evangelism. *Unlikely Converts* is another delightful read. If you want to be freshly amazed at God's power in the salvation of sinners, instructed in sharing the gospel with courage and clarity, and encouraged to faithfulness in your calling as an ambassador for Christ . . . this is the book for you!"
—**Mike McKinley**, pastor of Sterling Park Baptist Church and
author of *Am I Really a Christian?*

T0035179

"This book will be a massive help to me as I train my church family for evangelism in the twenty-first century. Why do I trust Randy Newman like no one else? First, I trust his theology: he knows the gospel is that Jesus is Lord. Second, I trust his anthropology: he knows how it feels during evangelism to be human and afraid. Third, I trust his historical and cultural engagement: he gets where we are at. And lastly, I trust his experience: he's been immersed in evangelism with coworkers, family, and friends for over thirty years. I am so grateful to God for this great gift to the church."

—**Rico Tice**, senior minister of evangelism at All Souls Church, London, and coauthor of *Christianity Explored*

"We need this book. Not because its author is a gospel guru, but because he's so much like us: a timid evangelist. Randy Newman writes that he can't remember sharing the gospel without fear, but that hasn't stopped his mouth or iced his heart. Few combine the heart for the lost, the patient ear, and the tongue of grace like Randy. He shows us how to let our speech always be gracious while still feeling unceasing anguish about hell-bound friends and family made in God's image. Let a brother who knows reluctance help you walk faithfully forward in yours."

—**David Mathis**, executive editor at Desiring God, pastor of Cities Church, Minneapolis/St. Paul, and author of *Habits of Grace*

UNLIKELY CONVERTS

Also by Randy Newman
Questioning Evangelism
Corner Conversations
Bringing the Gospel Home
Engaging with Jewish People

UNLIKELY CONVERTS

CONVERTS

IMPROBABLE STORIES OF FAITH
AND WHAT THEY TEACH US
ABOUT EVANGELISM

RANDY NEWMAN

KREGEL
PUBLICATIONS

Unlikely Converts: Improbable Stories of Faith and What They Teach Us About Evangelism
© 2019, 2024 by Randy Newman

Published by Kregel Publications, a division of Kregel Inc., 2450 Oak Industrial Dr. NE, Grand Rapids, MI 49505.

ISBN 978-0-8254-4888-1, print

Printed in the United States of America
24 25 26 27 28 29 30 / 5 4 3 2 1

Dedicated
to the memory of my father,
Marty Newman,
a most unlikely convert
who came to faith in the Messiah
a few short years before his death at age ninety

CONTENTS

ACKNOWLEDGMENTS

I thank my God at every remembrance of the many new believers who patiently told me their stories and answered my many questions about their paths to faith. They sacrificed time, energy, and, in many cases, tissues as they recalled emotional moments of God's power and rescue.

I'm deeply grateful for the friends who read portions of the book and offered helpful insights. Spencer Brand, Mark Petersburg, Patrick Dennis, Ben Hein, Jake Fritzke, and Bill Kynes all helped make this a better book.

My professors at Trinity Evangelical Divinity School challenged me and cheered me on as I pursued the research toward my doctorate, which sparked the beginnings of this book. I'm especially indebted to my dissertation committee—Craig Ott, Rick Richardson, and Harold Netland—for their dual commitments to academic excellence and the glory of God.

My good friend Diane Boucher spent seemingly hundreds of hours transcribing the interviews and told me many times how thankful she was for the front-row seat to such marvelous stories. She deserves a PhD in servanthood.

Many friends prayed me through the process of research and writing and kept reminding me of God's call to put into writing the stories I'd heard. I'm surrounded by supportive friends at our community group from McLean Presbyterian Church and my co-laborers in the gospel at The C. S. Lewis Institute.

Once again, I'm delighted to have the opportunity to work with Dennis Hillman and all the staff at Kregel Publications. They mix professionalism and personal care in joyful ways.

Most of all, I'm thankful for my wife, Pam, and her patience and love throughout the writing of this book, the seminary work that preceded it, and all the days of our marriage. She believed in me when I had doubts, listened to me brainstorm ideas (both good and ridiculous), and celebrated many milestones along the way. By God's grace, we still make each other laugh a lot.

PROLOGUE

Don't you just love stories? We sit on the edge of our seats to hear them. We download podcasts that feature them. We pay money to hear comedians tell funny ones. We wake up when a longwinded speaker breaks from explanations, elaborations, and emendations and says, "This reminds me of a story."

Stories form the backbone of this book. I retell how individuals' narratives intersect with the grandest story of all—the gospel. Allow me to begin with one of my favorites. It's about Lawrence and the pigs. If I were a betting man, I wouldn't have put a lot of money on Lawrence's ever attending a Bible study. In fact, I would have wagered against his ever going to *anything* connected with faith or God or the Bible. Like all the people I write about in this book, Lawrence was an unlikely candidate for a Christian convert. But in his freshman year in college, Lawrence did go to an event where students could ask "some Bible expert" any question they wanted. Lawrence went because he heard there'd be pizza. And the girl who invited him gave out cookies to anyone who said they'd come.

He had virtually no church background to speak of. When he filled out the part of his college application that asked for his religion, he had to ask his mother what he should write. She told him, "Methodist," and that's what he wrote, although he had no idea what that meant. His mother had taken him to church a few times, but he doubted whether God existed. When I asked him how he would describe himself as he began college, he offered the words "lonely, angry, and apathetic."

So he went to the ask-the-expert event to be "obnoxious" and "have fun" and to try to show the speaker that the Christian faith had "obvious issues." What he remembers most was that the speaker and the Christians were nice to him even though he "was being really mean." He asked the speaker, "What about aliens? What does that mean for Christianity?" The speaker responded brilliantly, admitting he didn't know much about aliens, that he didn't think their existence would affect Christianity all that much, and that if Lawrence wanted to know about Christianity, he should attend the eight-week study of the gospel of Mark that would start the next week.

So Lawrence went, with an attitude of "whatever" (a word he used a lot during the first fifteen minutes of our conversation). He asked many questions during those eight weeks and was impressed that the leader answered thoughtfully and respectfully. He learned a lot about God's righteousness and his own sinfulness. For a few weeks, he was baffled about how "unfair" it was for Jesus to pay for his sins. But he found himself believing more and more as the weeks passed.

At one point in our conversation, I asked him if there were any major objections or questions that needed resolution. Was there a significant roadblock, I wondered, that, once removed, would pave the way for belief? He paused and shook his head no. But then he remembered and said, "Well . . . the thing that stands out in my head mostly . . . was about the pigs and Jesus casting the demons into the lake."

I must confess. At that point, I wanted to say, "Really? That tripped you up? Even if I wasn't Jewish with my innate disdain for pork, I'm not sure that's what would hold me back from God's offer of eternal life." I tried to clarify by asking, "What was your question about the pigs?"

His answer didn't help me much. "What the heck was that? Jesus just killed all those pigs? They didn't do anything." But then he just started laughing and made a face that seemed to say, "That story makes no sense." So I asked him how the leader answered his question, and Lawrence's laughter came to a sudden stop. He told me the Bible study leader took his question seriously and started by admitting that he wasn't sure. That impressed Lawrence as humble and sincere. And then he suggested there really must be some things that are evil, that we shouldn't mess around with demons, and there must be a big difference between being a pig and being a person.

I asked him if that satisfied him and he said it did. "I was amazed that he had an answer," he said and added, "people I had dealt with before in churches that I had been to didn't know how to handle the Bible." They just told him to believe in Jesus and stop asking all his questions. That didn't sit well with a fairly intelligent guy, and so he dismissed Christianity as a stupid person's religion. However, a thoughtful answer about pigs persuaded Lawrence that there probably were good answers for his other questions.

There's much more to his story, a beautiful and gradual one that included a lot more Bible studies, a major conference for Christian students, attending a good church where people *did* know how to handle the Bible, and a lot of conversations where he learned more and more about Jesus's "unfair" sacrifice for sinful people like Lawrence.

His experience highlights at least four important lessons:

First, the process of coming to Christ takes time. While God certainly can work instantaneously, most often he does not. People tend to come to faith gradually.

Second, God uses a large and diverse cast of ordinary people to accomplish his extraordinary purposes. People tend to come to faith communally.

> People's stories reveal a tapestry of experiences, struggles, realizations, and transformations.

Third, layers of dramas lie beneath the surface. People's stories reveal a tapestry of experiences, struggles, realizations, and transformations. People tend to come to faith variously.

Fourth, nothing is too difficult for God. He can and does draw people to himself miraculously. People *always* come to faith supernaturally.

My conversation with Lawrence was part of the dissertation research I conducted toward my doctorate. Hearing his story was just one of forty deeply moving and exciting experiences I had along the way. I know: we don't usually expect the words "dissertation" and "exciting" to appear within a thousand paragraphs of each other. But as I heard from recent converts about how God worked to transfer them from the domain of darkness to the realm of saving light, I went through a lot of tissues. I have since listened to several other conversion stories that weave their way into this book.

We Need Help Telling Our Story

I'm convinced that hearing people's stories can help us proclaim the gospel more fruitfully. Through this book, I hope to encourage you in that task. But let's be realistic—evangelism has never been easy, and that's not likely to change. Consider this scenario:

You've got new neighbors. And your pastor has convinced you to invite them to church. What could be a kinder gesture of "Welcome to the neighborhood" than an invitation to worship together? But you don't know if they're Christians. In fact, you'd almost bet they're not. You remember attending a training seminar years ago about how to present the gospel concisely, clearly, boldly, and sooner rather than later. Even though you cling firmly to the truth that people are lost apart from Christ, somehow, that all seems unhelpful at this moment.

You wonder what to say after "Hello" and before "Are you ready to become a Christian?" Most of us might think, "Oh, there's so much you can say." But we quickly admit we're not sure where to begin. This book aims to help with that task. Some refer to this as "pre-evangelism." I love that term, but to be honest, it's too vague because that can be a huge continuum. I hope this book clears up that vagueness, explores the many varieties of pre-evangelism, and offers specific strategies for knowing what to say, how to say it, when to build plausibility, which obstacles to overcome, and why a gradual approach may be better than saying everything at once.

Our World Needs Our Story

Our world has shifted dramatically in the past decade. Our old strategies for evangelism need significant retooling. Even in the few years since I wrote *Questioning Evangelism* (2004), our audience has moved further away from what used to be valid starting points of conversation.

Here's how I envision our current situation. Not long ago I was watching a hockey game and found myself equally enjoying the athletic skills of the players and the verbal dexterity of the announcer. He crafted sentences as brilliantly and spontaneously as the athletes passed and shot that tiny black disc while skating close to breakneck speed.

At one point the contest was horribly lopsided, with one team unable to clear the puck out of their zone for more than two minutes, an eternity in the world of hockey. The announcer screamed, "Here's another shot turned away by the goalie. But they can't clear. And now a slap shot from the point. Save. But they can't control the rebound. Here's another scorcher that goes wide. I can't believe it. They get a fifth shot in as many seconds. Finally the goalie hangs on and we get a break." And then he added, "It seems that the ice is tilted!"

Can you picture that? Tilted ice for a hockey game? Play with that image for just a moment. The two hockey teams come out of their respective locker rooms to skate around and warm up on the ice before the game. They notice, however, before stepping onto the playing surface, that one team is going to have a mammoth advantage over the other. The rink slants downhill in their favor. The other team will have to skate, pass, and shoot uphill.

If you can go with this bizarre illustration, I think you'll agree the teams (both of them since they switch sides after each period) should not even begin to play until the ice gets untilted.

In our world today, evangelistically speaking, the ice is tilted. And Christians are on the downhill side of the playing surface. Non-Christians feel like they have the upper hand—both intellectually and morally. We have work to do to untilt the ice before we start the "game" of evangelism. Pre-evangelism untilts the ice.

We've been moving in this post-Christian direction for quite some time. In fact, I believe the shift is woven into the very foundation of

American history. We're all familiar with this line in the Declaration of Independence: "We hold these truths to be self-evident . . ." But did you know that Thomas Jefferson's earlier draft of that phrase read, "We hold these truths to be sacred and undeniable"? It was Benjamin Franklin who bristled at the obviously religious flavor of that phrase. "Using heavy backslashes, he crossed out the last three words of Jefferson's phrase . . . and changed it to read: 'We hold these truths to be self-evident.'"[1] The very trajectory of America's national identity pointed toward self-autonomy and away from submission to God.

We need to realize that time deepens the problem. I believe we can see cultural, spiritual parallels to physicist Max Planck's observations about science: "A new scientific truth does not triumph by convincing its opponents and making them see the light, but rather because its opponents eventually die, and a new generation grows up that is familiar with it."[2]

Please don't get bogged down in the historical roots or precedents for our current cultural malaise. It has not been a steady slide without major explosions along the way. The 1960s, for instance, provided a cultural earthquake with aftershocks, counterreactions, and reverberations that continue to shake us.

However we got here, as proclaimers of the good news, we need to "understand the times" (cf. 1 Chron. 12:32) and know how to "become all things to all people so that by all possible means [we] might save some" (1 Cor. 9:22). Most people today are not predisposed positively toward the gospel. They're not "ready to receive Christ." Many do not feel all that positive about God. As I heard a comedian put it, "I believe in God but I'm not a fan." Or, as *Atlantic Monthly* journalist Jonathan Rausch confessed, "I used to call myself an atheist and I still don't believe in God, but the larger truth is that it has been years since I really cared one way or another. I'm . . . an apatheist."[3]

Pre-Evangelism: The Help We Need

Fifty years ago, Francis Schaeffer, the one-of-a-kind preacher and evangelist in postmodern Europe (before most people ever heard the term *postmodern*) told us, "Pre-evangelism is no soft option."[4] More recently, Russell Moore awakened us to the reality that "we can stop counting on the culture to do pre-evangelism" for us.[5]

The fact that Tim Keller felt the need to write a prequel to his book *The Reason for God* illustrates my point. This earlier book answered questions some non-Christians ask. But Keller found that many outsiders weren't asking any questions. In his preface to *Making Sense of God*, Keller says the former book "does not begin far back enough for many people. Some will not even begin the journey of exploration, because, frankly, Christianity does not seem relevant enough to be worth their while."[6]

We need to back up and start our evangelistic efforts with more fundamental discussions. I've heard people say the difference between Keller's first book and his more recent *Making Sense of God* is that the first one provides answers for people who have questions. The second one poses questions for people who think they already have answers. The first is for someone already wondering if there are good reasons to become a Christian. The second is for someone who doubts that any good reasons exist.

My prayer is that *Unlikely Converts* will help you know what to say to people, whether they're asking questions or not.

I've lived in the realm of pre-evangelism for quite some time. I came to faith in the Messiah from a secularized Jewish background after more than four years of gradually moving from "Are you crazy? Jews don't believe in Jesus," to "Hmm. Maybe I need to consider who that Jewish carpenter was," to "Don't tell anyone I'm reading the New Testament," to "My Lord and my God!" I benefited greatly from patient Christian friends who trusted our sovereign God to move me incrementally at his pace.

I also benefited from reading C. S. Lewis's *Mere Christianity*, perhaps the greatest model of pre-evangelism ever. When Lewis was asked to put together a series of radio broadcasts to explain the Christian faith to BBC listeners during World War II, he opted to spend the first several episodes on how we know what we know. Long before ever saying a word about God or Jesus or sin or the cross, he camped out on "right and wrong as a clue to the meaning of the universe." These brief weekly broadcasts eventually became the written book *Mere Christianity*, which many have called the most influential Christian book of the twentieth century. We now read four or five short chapters one after the other in just a few minutes, but their original presentation allowed for a week's worth of rumination after suggestive, pre-evangelistic, partial messages such as:

- "Human beings . . . have this curious idea that they ought to behave in a certain way."[7]
- "They do not in fact behave in that way."[8]
- "We have cause to be uneasy."[9]
- "God is our only comfort. He is also the supreme terror: the thing we most need and the thing we most want to hide from."[10]

In a letter to the BBC producers, Lewis explained, "It seems to me that the New Testament, by preaching repentance and forgiveness, always assumes an audience who already believe in the law of nature and know they have disobeyed it. In modern England we cannot at present assume this, and therefore most apologetics begins a stage too far on. The first step is to create, or recover, the sense of guilt. Hence if I gave a series of talks, I shd [*sic*] mention Christianity only at the end, and would prefer not to unmask my battery till then."[11]

I came to appreciate Lewis's approach even more when I began evangelistic ministry on the staff of Campus Crusade for Christ. I served for more than three decades on East Coast urban campuses where the typical evangelistic strategies that worked so well in Midwestern and Southern America didn't even cause people to blink. I had to learn pre-evangelistic strategies because my audiences didn't seem to care one whit about having a personal relationship with God.

The Biblical Case for Pre-Evangelism

I'm convinced that pre-evangelism is essential for reaching people with the gospel in postmodern settings today. But perhaps I need to make my case a bit more persuasively. After all, isn't the gospel self-authenticating and powerful enough on its own? Do we really need to appeal to fallen people's inadequate reasoning in proclaiming a message about rebirth? Perhaps my quoting of Schaeffer, Moore, and Keller still leave you wanting input from a higher authority.

> The Scriptures offer a variety of preparations for the gospel before stating the message outright.

To be sure, proclaiming the gospel is powerful. We trust in the Holy Spirit, who "will prove the world to be in the wrong about sin and righteousness and judgment" (John 16:8) as we do so. But we must notice that the Scriptures offer a variety of preparations for the gospel before stating the message outright.

At this point, I must offer a few definitions. What exactly is evangelism, and how is pre-evangelism distinct from or related to evangelism? We need to be very clear about this. I hear a lot of fuzzy thinking about evangelism, and I'd hate to contribute to that fog. Here's how I am using these terms in this book.

Evangelism is the verbal proclamation of a very specific message: that Jesus died to atone for sins, that he rose from the dead, and that people must respond with repentance and faith. *Pre-evangelism* refers to the many different things that can pave the way for that proclamation. Evangelism and pre-evangelism are related, but we must remember their distinctions.

Sharing your testimony is a great pre-evangelistic strategy—but it's not evangelism. Discussing philosophical arguments for the existence of God may be exactly what you need to do with some skeptics—but it's not evangelism. Admiring beauty in nature or order in the physical universe and asking why our world seems so tailor-made for people is a very good pre-evangelistic tactic (one that I particularly love!)—but it's not evangelism. And digging wells or building houses or feeding hungry people might serve in pre-evangelistic ways—but that's not evangelism either.

I get nervous when people tell me they helped their neighbor with a chore around their house and then declare, "That's the gospel!" No it's not. It was probably a really great thing to do, and it may have even communicated sacrificial love to the neighbor. It might have even made them wonder why you're so nice. But until you use words that articulate some very important facts about the cross, you've only paved the way for evangelism. You haven't yet evangelized. We need to maintain the difference.

The distinction between evangelism and pre-evangelism has similarities with the distinction between conversion and the path that leads to that defining experience. Conversion is "our willing response to the gospel call, in which we sincerely repent of sins and place our trust in Christ for salvation."[12] A long process often precedes conversion. In this book, I will use the phrases "coming to faith" and "faith stories" to include both the specific event of conversion and the many things that lead up to that point.

Here is one significant argument in favor of the value of pre-evangelism: the entire Old Testament is pre-evangelistic. It paves the way for a message that, when finally presented, prompts a response of, "Ohhh. So that's what we've been waiting for!" (I have to wonder if that wasn't Simeon's feeling when he saw the infant Jesus in the temple—Luke 2:25–32.)

The first hint at a gospel of a suffering Messiah in Genesis 3:15 is remarkably cryptic and incomplete. God declares, "I will put enmity between you and the woman, and between your offspring and hers; he will crush your head, and you will strike his heel." Who's crushing whose head? And how does the striking of a heel compare? The text urges the reader to keep reading with the skills of a detective to see how that puzzling prediction will come to fulfillment. The drama of the Old Testament brings a dazzling array of characters onto the stage, prompting us to wonder which one could be the head crusher promised in the garden. The way Eve describes her newborn son makes us think that, just perhaps, he's the one (Gen. 4:1). But it doesn't take long for us to see he's no leading character for us to follow. The same can be said about Noah, who "found favor in the eyes of the LORD" (6:8). But he lets us down when he gets drunk (9:21). Might it be Abraham? We doubt it when he lies and says his wife is his sister—twice! (12:10–20; 20:1–12). And on and on it goes with disappointing non-Messiahs, one after another. And so we long for one who won't let us down. Can we not see this pattern of hope and disappointment as a form of pre-evangelism?

The Old Testament does far more to prepare our hearts for the Messiah than simply hint at his suffering; it moves us toward solving the mystery of who he will be. It features characters who act out intriguing dramas that seem to point forward to a main character who will make all the minidramas make more sense. Abraham offers up a son as a sacrifice but has the process halted by a God who provides his own substitute. The text itself lets us know this drama is not finished because it identifies the location as "The LORD Will Provide" (Gen. 22:14). You would have thought it should be called, "The Lord Did Provide." Apparently this drama pointed to a future provision that will be better.

So many examples could be given. One man, David, fights a battle against an enemy, Goliath, so that all who identify with him will be saved. While we could zoom our lens in on David's courage, the story is crafted in such a way that we see God's supernatural miracle as a way of saving his people through an unlikely representative. The Old Testament is filled with types, foreshadowings, predictions, and unfinished stories to prepare us for a message yet to come.

> Sometimes people need to consider ideas
> that pave the way for the core truths of the
> gospel before hearing those propositions.

Fair enough, you say. The Old Testament is pre-evangelistic. But we live after the cross. Now that the Messiah has come, we simply need to point to his finished cross-work and reap where the Old Testament has sown. Right? Not quite. The New Testament recounts instances of partial gospel proclamations. It gives us models and templates for pre-evangelism. I'll offer a few here, but I'll elaborate more throughout this book. Consider Jesus's tantalizing offer of "living water" while saving an explanation about atonement, the cross, and forgiveness for later (see John 4:1–39). Or think about Jesus's questions to the rich man that led to a list of commandments (a rather select list at that!) but no discussion of salvation by faith alone (see Mark 10:17–22). Or examine Paul's sermon in Athens, which went for quite a while, meandering into quotes of pagan poets, before saying anything about a resurrection (see Acts 17:16–34). Sometimes people need to consider ideas that pave the way for the core truths of the gospel before hearing those propositions, and the Bible gives us models of what that can look and sound like.

This Book's Approach

You may be surprised to know that I'm not one of those bold evangelists who always shares the gospel with people on airplanes. In fact, as I'm boarding, I often pray for God to provide an empty seat next to me so I can just read or take a nap. When I began serving with The C. S. Lewis Institute, they offered to provide me with business cards with my title as Senior Teaching Fellow for Apologetics and Evangelism. I requested something more C. S. Lewisian: The Most Reluctant Evangelist. They printed their option.

I struggle with evangelism. I've learned a lot from Campus Crusade's founder and president Bill Bright's book *Witnessing Without Fear*. But in my library, because of its title, I shelve that book under Fiction. I can't remember ever witnessing without fear. And for that reason, I believe God uses me in encouraging fellow reluctant evangelists with the task of proclaiming good news when we'd all rather put in earbuds and listen to podcasts.

If I may adapt C. S. Lewis's words from his introduction to *Reflections on the Psalms*, I believe I can help nonevangelists because, like them, I am not an expert. Lewis wrote: "I write for the unlearned about things in which I am unlearned myself. . . . It often happens that two schoolboys can solve difficulties in their work for one another better than the master can. When you took the problem to a master, as we all remember, he was very likely to explain what you understood already, to add a great deal of information which you didn't want, and say nothing at all about the thing that was puzzling you. . . . The fellow-pupil can help more than the master because he knows less."[13]

I'm hoping my status as "fellow-pupil" can help you reach out to the non-Christians God has sovereignly placed around you. Thankfully, I have found that those of us who are nonevangelists find the components of pre-evangelism more suited to our natures. Some will say we're simply chickening out. And in many instances, perhaps we are. But, putting the matter in the best light, I have seen that in some cases God uses timid nonevangelists in the pre-evangelistic portion of the process, in ways uniquely suited to their gifts and callings.

Brainstorms

Christians often wonder, "What should I say to someone who says . . ." and then they offer a difficult scenario to respond to. They want to know *the* right thing to say that will be impossible to refute. But most of us can't think that quickly or dazzle that powerfully. In fact, I'm not sure that's the best tactic. We want to engage more than amaze.

Brainstorming, I think, is a better way to prepare ourselves for evangelistic and pre-evangelistic conversations. When we try to come up with just one response, it paralyzes us. When we try to come up with a dozen, we end up with two or three good things to say that can work in a variety of situations. Besides, no two questioners are alike. What would make us think that one statement would fit every situation? Coming up with several possible responses prepares us for several possible situations.

Thus, I've suggested some brainstorms at the end of each chapter of this book, to stimulate your thinking. Don't think of these brainstorms as "*the* right way" or "magic bullets." I'm simply trying to spark your own brainstorming to help you prepare for a variety of opportunities.

An Invitation

I realize the task of evangelism can seem overwhelming. Even with all the nuanced ideas in this book, we can feel intimidated. My aim is to be practical. It's helpful to study philosophy and apologetics and societal trends, but often after reading those books, we wonder, "OK. But what do I say?" This book seeks to answer that question.

I was greatly encouraged to listen to the stories of the recent converts I interviewed. On several occasions, I cried. Quite often, I found myself marveling at how the unlikeliest of stories unfolded. God works in the realm of the impossible. I hope my retelling those stories will embolden you to play your part in the evangelism process and plead with God to do his part.

PART 1

How People Come to Faith

CHAPTER 1

Gradually

A bizarre cult ensnared Joni's parents for most of their lives. Through her first seventeen years, Joni thought their religion was normal. They went to something like a church, sat under convoluted messages from a leader who had convinced his followers he was the messiah. She watched her parents hang on every word, but "it never really made sense" to her.

Part of this cult's practice was for the church's leader to match up men and women to be married. Joni's parents met each other on their wedding day. Their leader determined they would make a good couple and now, twenty-plus years later, they were still together. But Joni said most of the marriages she saw in her church were horrible. Haltingly she told me, "My mom didn't want to be a mom. She didn't enjoy raising kids, and—I definitely felt like I wasn't a source of joy for my parents. I was nothing more than a disappointment to my parents."

Joni began to have horrible visions of her own future when her father began to talk about whom he would match her up with for her marriage partner. (As the church had grown—to over a hundred thousand members worldwide!—marriages were now arranged by parents rather than the leader.) So at age seventeen, Joni ran away from home.

You might think, "Oh good. She got away from that madness." Unfortunately, she ran into different madness—the kind a young, attractive woman often finds in a world filled with a variety of ills. She was sexually exploited, became addicted to various drugs, and moved from one temporary-living mess to another.

Miraculously, she got accepted to a prestigious college with scholarship housing on campus. Dorm life may have been the most stable living situation she ever experienced. It was there that she met some Christians, whose friendliness prompted deeply conflicted feelings.

They were remarkably nice people, but her attitudes toward God and religion were, understandably, quite negative. "My life was ruined by religion," she told me, with anger in her voice. "It was the thing I resented more than anything else. I had wholly and completely rejected the idea of aligning myself with a certain religion . . . because it was something I very much feared."

> Like so many of the stories I heard, Joni's path to saving faith progressed gradually.

Being enrolled in a major university allowed Joni to find help from the school's counseling service. As you can well imagine, she battled depression, anxiety, and other struggles. But it was her newly forming friendships with Christians, she says, that made the biggest difference. They were kind and showed interest in her. She found great friendship in a woman who served as a campus ministry intern. Every time she mentioned her name to me, her face beamed with a delightful smile.

"Our conversations were like an open forum that I never experienced before, where I was allowed to ask questions and state doubts. I was never allowed to do that when I was growing up in my parents' faith."

Like so many of the stories I heard, Joni's path to saving faith progressed gradually. Many conversations with the campus ministry intern, late-night conversations with friends about the Bible, a weekend retreat, listening to sermons at a good church, and writing a lot in her journal moved her along incrementally from resentment to reception.

Telling me about rereading parts of her journal, Joni said, "I noticed this very gradual shift in my note taking. I was always comparing what I was hearing and what I was learning to what I had been taught in my parents' church." She told how she began to understand why Jesus died on the cross (something her parents' church said was a tragic mistake), that he paid for sins, and that he made people new creatures.

And then, in a moment I'll never forget, she paused and very deliberately stated, "I had done all of these things and made all these mistakes and screwed up on so many levels. And to be totally and wholly forgiven for these things by God was a huge experience for me." Sitting outside a coffee shop with a lot of people walking nearby, she began to cry. So did I. Eventually, tearfully, she whispered, "The word 'gratitude' doesn't even begin to describe it."

"A Very Gradual Shift"

Let's consider Joni's description of her experience—"I noticed this very gradual shift." Many of the people I interviewed echoed her sentiment. Some described it as a series of intellectual realizations. Others described a melting of anger. A few expressed a sadness that "maybe my friends are right and I've been a jerk for the way I've been making fun of them." One guy just laughed as he recounted his embarrassment when he realized that his best arguments against the gospel were lame.

Miles, a lacrosse player at a large university, told me he attended a series of discussions about sex from a biblical perspective that convinced him he should break up with his girlfriend. Actually, he didn't want to break up; he just thought they should stop having sex. She broke up with him when he told her of his decision. After the breakup, he started attending an evangelistic Bible study.

(By the way, that's not what they called it. Wouldn't that be a nonstarter: "Hey, you want to attend an evangelistic Bible study?" They called it something like "organic discussion group." Miles couldn't remember the exact title. He just knew they talked a lot about Jesus.)

His progress—over the course of two semesters—could be summarized as follows:

1. "Christians are crazy. They don't have sex."
2. "Maybe waiting until you get married to have sex isn't such a bad idea. But it's not possible."
3. "OK. I hate not having sex, but I think it's the right thing to do."
4. "I've got to think about something other than sex."
5. "I never knew Jesus said all those things."
6. "Oh, so *that's* why Christians make such a huge deal about Easter."

One night, while eating dinner with his teammates, he found himself defending his decision to not have sex until marriage. They laughed hysterically and blasted him with questions. He told me, as he answered them, he found himself amazed at hearing the words coming out of his mouth. It was while talking to them about sex that he realized he now believed what they taught at the Bible study about Jesus. It was a long, gradual process that culminated in telling others what was occurring inside.

Several campus ministers with whom I've worked know this intuitively: coming to faith often occurs gradually. There may have been a time, decades ago, when we could assume, "People are ready to receive Christ; they just have to be invited to make a decision." I'm not convinced we should have ever assumed that, but most assuredly those days are long gone.

Two long-time campus ministers, Don Everts and Doug Schaupp, wrote an entire book about gradual conversion, breaking the process down into "five thresholds of postmodern conversion." They said the students moved

1. "from distrust to trust";
2. then "from complacent to curious";
3. then "from being closed to change to being open to change in their life";
4. then "from meandering to seeking"; and,
5. finally, "they needed to cross the threshold of the kingdom itself."[1]

Their observations are quite helpful, and their term "threshold" adequately describes many people's experiences. But not all. I simply want to tweak their theory to say there may be many varieties of threshold series. Some series have five thresholds; some have three; and some thresholds may not seem as distinct or separate from each other as Everts and Schaupp seem to imply. And for some, "thresholds" might not be the best term at all. For some they're epiphanies, or discoveries, or surrenders, or embracings, or mini-decisions. The important point is for us to allow for and adapt to a gradual approach in how we help people move along at the pace and prompting of the Holy Spirit.

From A to Z

Here's one way to think of this. Visualize a line with the alphabet written above it. Consider this a scale of unbelief from A to Z, with A being the hardest atheist you can imagine and Z being someone ready to become a Christian. Every non-Christian we meet fits on that line somewhere.[2] For people who already believe in God, think the Bible is probably worth listening to, and are already convinced they need forgiveness for some things they've done, starting a conversation somewhere around letter T seems best. Helping someone move from T to Z can begin with a question like, "If you were to die tonight, how sure are you that you'd go to heaven?" For someone at letter D, that question might sound bizarre or annoying or incoherent.

Worst of all, the "dying tonight" question might strike some as arrogant or unrealistically confident. Consider *New Yorker* columnist Adam Gopnik's insight from his introduction to a book about the Bible: "Our ancestors acknowledged doubt while practicing faith. We moderns are drawn to faith while practicing doubt."[3] If he's right, and I'm pretty sure he is, many of the individuals we meet have more doubt than faith and more questions than answers. They're more likely to say, "What makes you so sure?" than "Please tell me more."

We need a variety of starting points for people with a variety of beliefs. For people at the beginning of the alphabet, letters A through E, we might begin with open-ended questions like "Do you ever think much about spiritual things?" or "Do you like to read? What authors have shaped your thinking the most?" For people in the middle of the alphabet, perhaps letters H through N, we might try "I wonder if you'd ever be interested in coming to a Bible study I go to?" or "Are you guys looking for a church to go to this Christmas?"

As I hope you can surmise, this isn't an exact science. Wouldn't it be nice if someone developed an evangelistic app for your phone that would tell you what letter best fits the person you're talking to? It would pick up vibes from them, analyze their level of gospel receptivity, and then suggest appropriate questions to ask or provocative statements to make. It could serve as an evangelistic Geiger counter!

> If we develop excellent communication skills, we can adapt our pre-evangelistic approaches to a variety of people with a wide range of attitudes or objections to our message.

A better approach would be to ask questions and listen carefully to people's responses—both the words they say and the expressions they make. If we develop excellent communication skills, we can adapt our pre-evangelistic approaches to a variety of people with a wide range of attitudes or objections to our message. I believe this is one application of what Paul wrote in his phrase "so that you may know how to answer everyone" at the end of Colossians 4:6. I'll say more about that important passage in chapter 7.

Biblical Support for Gradual Pre-Evangelism

I've already mentioned Paul's speech on Mars Hill as recorded in Acts 17. Most scholars acknowledge that Luke only gave us highlights of the speech rather than the entire text. In that day, orators spoke for an hour or more in such settings, and Paul's message probably fit that pattern.[4] It is fair to ask the key question, "Was Paul making a big mistake with such a long philosophical argument?" I don't think he was (and I've found support for this interpretation in the majority of evangelical commentaries).

First, it would seem odd, to say the least, that God would inspire his Word to give us something that would take so long to read if Paul shouldn't have taken so long to say it. Further, the account reads like other records of gospel preaching in Acts, complete with a report of mixed responses. Some sneered, some wanted to hear more, and some believed. In fact, the report about Athens sounds even better than others because we're given specific names of people who believed. I take it that Luke thought this outreach might have actually been *more* successful than some others. He goes out of his way to tell us that one of the converts, Dionysius, was "a member of the Areopagus," thus not the most likely of positive responders. Another, Damaris, was a woman, thus someone who had to hear the message second- or thirdhand. (Women were not allowed at such gatherings in that culture.) If anything, Paul's method of building his case gradually is heralded as brilliant, not mistaken.

We would be wise to copy his example in our day. Our culture resembles Athens (steeped in skepticism and shaped by secularism) far more than Jerusalem (aware of God's holiness and convinced of people's sinfulness).

Consider Paul's approach. He wanted his audience to open up to the reality that we are created to know God and find our meaning in him. He quoted some of their poets to bolster his case: "As some of your own poets have said, 'We are his offspring'" (Acts 17:28). Then notice Paul's progression of thought. He moved from what they already knew or accepted to what he wanted them to understand and receive.

If he had been preaching in a synagogue in Jerusalem, he might have progressed as follows:

1. God created us in his image. We know this from the Scriptures.
2. He's not a material god like the ones the Athenians worship.

3. Therefore, we can surmise that we are not merely material beings.
4. We can conclude that we're made to connect spiritually to a spiritual God.

But Paul takes a different route:

1. We are God's offspring. Even your poets recognize this truth.
2. From that, we surmise that we are not merely material beings.
3. Therefore, God is not merely material "like gold or silver or stone" (Acts 17:29).
4. We conclude that we're made to know a personal God in a personal way to fulfill our personal nature.

Whether you follow all the nuances of Paul's lines of argument (or my interpretations of them), I hope you can value his gradual approach. For some conversations, we need to start at the point where we challenge people's assumptions about truth before we proclaim *the* truth. We might need to soften their hardness against the possibility of knowing God before we tell them of the joys of knowing that God. In many, perhaps most conversations, we need to suggest that some parts of our inner being are not what they should be before we proclaim that "all have sinned and fall short of the glory of God" (Rom. 3:23).

G. K. Chesterton followed Paul's example in his influential work *The Everlasting Man*. He spent the first half of that book discussing the nature of man before discussing the nature of one very significant man, "the everlasting man," Jesus. Actually, he backed up even further. Before discussing what we know about people, Chesterton challenged his readers to consider what we know about anything—about ourselves, about truth, and ultimately, about God. In the very introduction he invited his audience to first step outside Christianity by looking at it rationally before stepping inside Christianity and believing it by faith. To use his terms, his approach was "historical rather than theological."[5]

Varieties of Pre-Evangelistic Experiences

So how do we do this? I'll suggest a few ways, with the hope they spark many other ideas.

We believe there is only one way to God, through Jesus's atonement on the cross. Our gospel message is an exclusive one. We take seriously Jesus's uncompromising declaration, "No one comes to the Father except through me" (John 14:6). However, there may be many starting points before we get to that exclusive gospel message.

The most straightforward route consists of a protracted gospel presentation with stops along the way to see if people understand what we've said so far. In some instances, it is wise to simply present the gospel concisely and clearly through some form of a four-point outline. We have many versions to choose from but they all tend to rest on four key pillars.

Our message includes two important truths about each of these:

1. God: he's holy and he's loving.
2. People: we're made in God's image, but we've rebelled against him.
3. Jesus: he died a sacrificial death to pay for our sins, and he rose again.
4. How we must respond: with repentance and with faith.

This is easy to memorize and state without taking a lot of time. But each point requires clarification or defense or elaboration. For some people, the sticking point is at the very beginning. If they don't believe in God, the rest of our four-point outline makes little sense. They may say, "This is nice. If I believed in God, I might consider what you're saying. But I don't believe in God. I don't believe in unicorns either." So we might have to stop at point one and engage in a tailor-made conversation before moving on to point two. They may not say anything at all. In those instances, we should ask more questions before simply forging ahead with our pre-scripted, one-size-fits-all soliloquy.

Recently, some have proposed a more narrative four-point outline for sharing the gospel.[6] It points people to the story line of the Bible and calls for a response as follows:

1. Creation: The world we live in was created by a personal God who designed it as good, orderly, and beautiful.
2. Fall: People messed that up by rebelling against the Creator.
3. Redemption: God initiated a rescue by sending his Son to redeem and forgive rebellious people and start restoring the original created design.
4. Consummation: Eventually that process will be complete, and all the world will be renewed. Until then, we need to respond to God's offer of rescue by repenting and trusting God to start the renewal process in us.

Both approaches have strengths and weaknesses. The first one (God/People/Jesus/Response) has the strength of emphasizing our problem and the need for each individual to respond. But it can seem totally individualistic without any concern for the rest of the world. The second approach (Creation/Fall/Redemption/Consummation) fits more with the shape of the Bible as God has inspired it, but it can seem less urgent to individuals. It might seem nice to join God in his project to clean up the planet but not necessary for us to escape God's wrath.

Matt Chandler refers to these two presentations as "the gospel on the ground" and "the gospel in the air." He makes a convincing case that both can be used effectively to help lost people find salvation. "Both are necessary in order to begin to glimpse the size and the weight of the good news, the eternity-spanning wonderment of the finished work of Christ. Both are necessary so that we are not reductionistic in how we define what God is up to both in our hearts and in the universe around us."[7]

Here are a few routes of pre-evangelism worth exploring.[8] I heard some of these woven into the faith stories of my interviewees. I encourage you to experiment with them. I'm going to state these as concisely as possible for the sake of helping you grasp them.

When you craft a conversation (or, better yet, a series of conversations) around these lines, you'll want to move slowly. Think of these as road maps. It's important to look at a map before you drive from New York to Los Angeles to get the plan in your head. You can usually grasp it in just a few minutes. But actually making the drive will take a bit longer.

Note that these are not gospel presentations as the two examples above were. Rather, these merely prepare the way for a gospel presentation.

Route 1: Not That, nor That, but This
This approach can be very helpful when addressing the issue of *identity*.

- In what could be called "traditional cultures," people tend to build their identities on others. What your parents or your ethnic community or group of friends believe about you shapes how you think of yourself.
- In what might be called "modern cultures," people build their identities on themselves—their values, their goals, their gender, their passion, etc. As a bumper sticker expresses it, "Life isn't about finding yourself. Life is about creating yourself."
- Both of these approaches have problems.
  - Building your identity on others leads to insecurity, instability, guilt, shame, condemnation, or an insatiable need to please an ever-morphing audience.
  - But building your identity from within is confusing. (Which parts of yourself do you use, and which do you ignore?) Or it can be destructive. (If you're honest, when you look inside, you see a mix of good and bad. Building your life on some of your desires could ruin your life.) It can also be crushing if you can't live up to the standards you set for myself. And it can be downright depressing as you grow older and diminish in the ability to even come close to your goals, dreams, and hopes.

- But if you build your identity on someone who will
  - hold you to the highest standards, even higher than the ones you set for yourself,
  - while accepting and loving you when you fail by providing forgiveness and cleansing,
  - and give you a new identity that's better than one you could construct for yourself . . .

  that would be an identity worth having.

Route 2: Tension and Release

This approach can be very helpful when addressing the issue of *evil and suffering.*

- There's a lot of good in our world—beauty in nature, captivating music, intriguing works of art, etc.
- There's also a lot of ugliness—death, disease, decay, etc.
- We see both good and bad in people.
- We see both good and evil in ourselves. (Sometimes I say nice things to people; sometimes I'm glad people can't read my mind.)
- This conflict between good and bad can point us to God. He made our world good and he made us to know him and his goodness. But something has obviously gone wrong.
- We want to know this God sometimes, but at other times, we would rather he leave us alone.
- This creates a tension. Something inside us longs for resolution. We want to know the beauty and we want God to punish evil.
- The cross satisfies God's goodness and his judgment.

Route 3: Yes, but No, but Yes

This approach can be helpful when addressing the issue of *sexuality.*

- There are a lot of things in life that are really great. One might even call them "blessings."
- One really great thing is sex. It's pleasurable and profound.
- Yes, there's good reason why we value sex so much.

- But no, it cannot be the most important thing in life. It's a good gift but it's not a good god. (A lot of elaboration or explanation could be inserted here.)
- If we have God as the ultimate priority in our lives, his gifts fit in well. He's the one who designed sex to be as pleasurable and as profound as it is—or as it can be.
- Yes, sex can be what God wants it to be in our lives—if we get our priorities right.

Route 4: What If . . .
This approach can be very helpful when addressing the issue of *desires or longings.*[9]

- We all long for something more. It might be more joy or happiness or fun or meaning or significance or many other things.
- We are constantly disappointed.
- There are some things that seem to promise what we're looking for: falling in love, seeing a beautiful sunset, relishing a delicious meal, hearing a mesmerizing piece of music, etc.
- But even these experiences leave us disappointed.
- We could keep chasing other experiences, hoping to find one that doesn't let us down.
- Or we could become cynical and give up hope of ever finding anything more.
- But what if there was satisfaction somewhere? What if we don't have to settle for cynicism? What if the disappointments were never meant to satisfy but were only meant as pointers?
- What if we were meant for another world?

In the advance of God's kingdom . . . we do play a part, but we're not the main character. We are part of the process, but we're not the one who determines the timing.

There are other routes of pre-evangelism to explore. Doing so would require a willingness to experiment and a trust that God is in charge of the process. It would display a reliance on the Holy Spirit and a proper view of our limited role in the advance of God's kingdom. We do play a part, but we're not the main character. We are part of the process, but we're not the one who determines the timing.

Our Attitudes in Gradual Pre-Evangelism

Not long ago, I was interviewed on a live radio program about evangelism. The host told me about his career in sales, where he learned to "A-B-C: Always Be Closing." He elaborated that he always wanted to press his client for a decision. It was important, he assured me, to not let them walk away without "closing the deal." He then asked the leading question, "Don't you think we need to do the same thing with sharing the gospel? Shouldn't we always be closing?"

I must confess that I was not too happy at that moment. I feared his live radio show was about to suffer a kind of death. I tentatively countered, "Well . . . I do think we can learn a lot from the world of sales. I know I have taken some lessons from how sales people ask questions and offer their product. But I don't think evangelism is exactly like sales, and I don't think the gospel is a product."

There was a brief pause, followed by a change in topic. Something tells me I may not get invited back on that show again. This gradual approach to pre-evangelism that I'm promoting may require a shift in attitude. For those of us who have been trained to evangelize more quickly and "close the deal," we may need a change in perspective. I've made that shift. I've seen enough examples of God's use of the gradual approach to convince me it's worth our consideration and experimentation.

Here are three attitude adjustments I think can help us as we reach out in our Athens-like cultures.

1. Intentionally Rely on the Holy Spirit

This may seem obvious. We trust the Holy Spirit to open up blind eyes and soften hardened hearts. We realize the Holy Spirit must do the work of regeneration in order for our gospel proclamation to bear fruit. But are we willing to allow him to dictate the pace of the process as well? Sometimes he moves more slowly than we'd like. I find it helpful to pray in two directions throughout the outreach process. I pray for the non-Christian, that God would do what only he can do and make his gospel irresistible to them. But I also pray for myself, that God would give me peace in the midst of my anxiousness, and patience if the process doesn't move along as fast as I'd like. The same Holy Spirit who "will prove the world to be in the wrong about sin and righteousness and judgment" (John 16:8) in non-Christians, promises the fruit of the Spirit—which includes patience—in me.

2. Acknowledge That We Might Accomplish More by Attempting Less

This seems counterintuitive. We want to convince atheists that God really does exist, that he's holy and loving, that he wants us to know him personally, that he sent his Son so we could escape his wrath, and that they'd better say yes to the offer of forgiveness of sins right now because "today is the day of salvation!" But if we overwhelm people with too much information or arguments or "proofs," we might end up doing very little. We might do better by going for just one small goal at a time.

3. Be Willing to Remain Uncomfortable

A gradual approach to pre-evangelism might require some conversations to pause without resolution. To be sure, we'll want to suggest and offer the resolution later on. But we have to allow that uneasiness to linger long enough for them to feel the need for resolution. Otherwise our "answer" doesn't really connect to a real question they should be asking. For example, if we've persuaded someone that God is both holy and loving and we are both image-bearers and sinners, they might feel uneasy about all that. To quote C. S. Lewis again, "we have cause to be uneasy."[10] The gospel has to be bad news before it's good news. Sometimes we have to destabilize before offering a better way.

By the way, we might need to admit that some of our evangelistic strategies center more on feeling good about ourselves than on what's best for the non-Christian. Sometimes, we're more concerned about alleviating guilt feelings, or getting credit for proclaiming the whole gospel, or looking good before other believers than we are about promoting God's glory, following his timing, allowing for him to use others in the process, and trusting that he's more than capable of orchestrating his salvation process according to his timing and plan.

When I began my research project and wanted to recruit recent converts for my interviews, I spoke to a campus fellowship and asked for volunteers. "If you've become a Christian within the past two years, please sign up on this form I'm about to pass around." It seemed straightforward enough. I added, "I should tell you, however, that I probably won't be able to contact you for six months or more. So please be patient."

As the clipboard made its way up and down the rows, one young man, Matt, signed up—much to the surprise of his friend, Ben, sitting next to him. The two of them had been talking for quite some time about the gospel, and as far as Ben knew, Matt was still on the fence and had not yet come to faith. Later, Ben told me his conversation with Matt went something like this:

Ben: Hey, I noticed you signed up on that list to do that interview for the speaker.

Matt: Yeah.

Ben: I was kind of surprised by that. Did you become a Christian while that guy was talking?

Matt: No.

Ben: Well, then, did you become a Christian sometime since we talked on Tuesday?

Matt: No.

Ben: Am I missing something?

Matt: No. The guy said we should sign up if we've become a Christian, but he said he won't be able to get back in touch with us for six months. I'm pretty sure I'll be a Christian by then.

Ben told me, one year later, that Matt had indeed become a Christian—around six months after I spoke on their campus! Who would have ever thought that asking people to forecast belief could be part of their faith story? I never thought of "predictive evangelism" as a successful strategy.

But God often moves gradually—at his pace, through his processes, in unlikely, unpredictable, unscriptable, unimagined ways. Let's trust him with the process and his power to use us in improbable, wonder-filled ways.

BRAINSTORMS: STARTERS

We all need a few gospel conversation starters. It's worth brainstorming possibilities ahead of time. Ask yourself, what might work for you as go-to statements that help you transition from ordinary, casual conversations to eternally significant ones. Find words you'll feel comfortable saying. They need to sound like you, not like someone else you're parroting.

After finding out where people come from, what they do for an occupation, how they like to spend their free time, and so forth, you might try one of these:

- Was religion part of your upbringing? How has that shaped you today?
- Do you ever find yourself wondering about God or some of life's big questions?
- What kinds of things give you a sense of meaning or purpose?
- Do you ever think much about spiritual things?
- What part has faith ever played in your life?

CHAPTER 2

Communally

Thalia loved to make fun of her Christian friends. Her dorm room walls displayed profanity-laden posters she enjoyed quoting when around Christians. She loved to swear colorfully to embarrass them. During our conversation, she told me she once called a Christian friend and said, "Guess what! I've accepted Jesus into my life." When he replied excitedly, "Really?" she told me she said "'No,' and I laughed at him and cursed him out, calling him stupid and worse stuff. I was really horrible to him." Now, just a few years later, she shook her head in disbelief at her cruelty.

People craft their stories differently. Some move along chronologically. Some focus inwardly through a maze of emotions. Others outline intellectually the questions they needed to answer. Thalia's story hung on a sequence of people who came in and out of her life. Each one played a distinct role in her move from antagonism to acceptance. In addition to the high school friends she ridiculed, she also mentioned her mother.

"My low point was sitting in a courtroom watching my mom cry," she told me after listing her many alarming troubles due to drugs, alcohol, and car accidents. She continued, "At that point I just realized how my friends had led me to that path." She went off to college, determined not to get mixed up in the wrong crowd.

Her cast of characters also included "this one guy" who wasn't like any of the other Christians she had known. She paused and smiled at the remembrance of his part in her story. He didn't put up with her insults or mockery. He called her out for being so mean. And he challenged her to rethink her antagonism. He "asked me these little kernels of questions that would remain in the back of my head."

During her freshman year in college, while walking across campus, a woman handed her a card that said, "How do you know if you're going to heaven?" Her immediate reaction was "Jesus freak!" like the ones she'd made fun of back home. But then she thought, "Hey, this is my question!" She toyed with the idea of calling that Christian guy she respected back home. But then she thought, "'No. I don't want to call him. I didn't want anyone to know I was thinking about this."

She walked back to the woman handing out the cards and asked to discuss the topic of heaven. Intriguingly (to me, at least) the woman said she couldn't talk just then because she had all these cards she needed to hand out! They set up a time to meet, which turned into a series of meetings over the next few months. Her story beautifully wove together her one-on-one Bible studies with memories of conversations from years before.

I had already interviewed more than twenty people before meeting Thalia. Every story included friends, described as "so nice to me," "never judgmental," "patient with answering all my questions," "the sincerest people in the world," and so on. I was just about to endorse emphatically the truism, "You have to build a relationship before sharing the gospel." Sometimes people say, "You have to earn the right to be heard" or "People don't care how much you know until they know how much you care." Some even suggest a specific amount of time that "must" elapse before bringing up the topic of religion.

But then Thalia threw me a curve ball. While she did indeed hear the gospel from friends, it was a stranger who had the most impact. In fact, after our hour-long interview was over and I had put away my notebook and recorder, as we stood to shake hands and say good-bye, she added, "Hey, wait a minute. I just thought of something." (At that moment, I also thought of something: *Sorry. This interview is over! I've put away my notebook and recorder. You can't add anything more.*)

But she insisted. "It had to be anonymous," she said. I asked for clarification. She obliged: "I had alienated so many Christians that I just couldn't admit to them that I was interested. So it had to be a total stranger that I talked to about Jesus. It had to be anonymous."

> When I say that "coming to faith
> was a communal experience," I mean
> conversion came after interactions
> with a whole lot of people.

I went back and reread the transcripts of my previous interviews and had to admit that while friends played a significant role in people's faith stories, those friendships were often rather new when the gospel became the centerpiece of a relationship. The amount of time between "Hello" and "Let me tell you about Jesus" was a lot shorter than I had previously realized. Some said their very *first* encounter with a Christian included "Hey, how'd you like to come to church with me?"

A certain amount of trust can pave the way for better gospel conversations. I agree we should do all we can to conduct ourselves with "gentleness and respect" (1 Peter 3:15). But I fear that many of us, myself included, wait too long or demand too high a level of trust (which, by the way, is impossible to measure) before broaching the Jesus topic. By all means, let's pursue friendship, kindness, and trust. But let us also rely on the self-authenticating power of our message. Perhaps we should assume that God's word has already earned the right to be heard because of whose word it is!

The Voices of Others

I want to underline a key concept of this chapter and, in fact, this entire book. While most of the people I interviewed zoomed in on one particular relationship, they also spoke of input from a variety of other sources. When I say that "coming to faith was a communal experience," I mean conversion came after interactions with a whole

lot of people. They discussed the gospel with friends, heard numerous sermons (both live and online), read apologetic articles on the
web, went to small group Bible studies, heard total strangers' testimonies at meetings, and listened to podcasts. They heard a whole
chorus of voices singing different parts of the same song.

They also commented on hearing how the gospel shaped all of
life—their relationships, values, money, sex, and goals. I'll say more
about this in the next chapter. But I couldn't help but notice that
some spoke about how they were challenged to consider the Christian perspective on more levels than just "a relationship with God"
or "how to get to heaven." For some, the process began with a con-
frontation of what the Scriptures say about all relationships, or the
person's obsession with academic achievement, or his or her dreams
of making a lot of money, or numerous other not-so-pleasant topics.
While few would articulate it as such, their encounters with the gospel began as clashes between the one true God and their many idols.

Maria highlighted her need to see the gospel worked out in a variety of people's lives. It was good for her to hear why someone her
own age believed in Jesus. But it was also important for her to see it
in the lives of older people, and married people, and people with little children, and people with wild teenagers, and on and on the cast
of characters went. Maria saw all this in a church she attended for
several months before becoming a Christian and joining that church.

As an African American woman, she hesitantly told me that she
attended two different campus fellowships because "I'm just going
to be honest with you, one group was all Caucasian and the other
was black." Seeing the same faith lived out and expressed in two very
different cultures was what drew her in.

Maria took more time to tell me about one particular event than
any other part of her story. At a Christian student conference, she
attended a panel of pastors and their wives discussing how the gospel shaped their marriages. She excitedly told me, "It was just seeing how godly their relationships were and how they cared for one
another and loved one another . . . and especially how the wives
really did respect their husbands and were so encouraging to them

in the sense of supporting them in God's Word and the work that they do at home, and how the husbands would just lift up their wives and just praise them and what they did. To me, I thought that was beautiful."

Several women told me they were scared to pursue the gospel because of their strong feminist convictions. That whole "wives submit to your husbands" thing turned a lot of women off. Some benefited from hearing rational arguments about the logic of Ephesians 5. But more women said it was meeting married Christian women who seemed happy and respectful of their husbands that made the objection evaporate.

The Voices of Authors

I wondered if reading books played much of a part in people's faith stories. Were writers part of the chorus of voices who proclaimed the gospel? Yes and no. Some people devoured books. Some hardly read a word. And many fit somewhere in between. When I asked people if they had read any books while moving from unbelief to saving faith, the first twenty-five people all had the same answer: "Nah. Not really." (As an author, I found this rather discouraging.)

But then I started hearing some encouraging trends. Quite a few spoke of basic apologetics books that answered their questions. Lee Strobel's *The Case for Christ* and Tim Keller's *The Reason for God* received the most votes. One woman told me she read an eight-hundred-page systematic theology seminary textbook. (She had a lot of questions.)

We just never know who will read and who won't. We should offer books, suggest website articles, narrow down recommendations to specific chapters, and not give up on the written word. We shouldn't be surprised if people don't read what we give them, but we shouldn't abandon the powerful tool of the written word.

Two Encouraging Examples

Louis said he never read anything before becoming a Christian but then began reading after his conversion. Allen read tons of books before conversion, and they led him away from God. But then one very specific book brought him back.

When I asked Louis my standard "Did you read any books" question, his answer was more emphatic than the "Nah, not really" variety of answer. "No. Absolutely not," he told me. "I was practically illiterate. But after I became a Christian, I started reading a lot." "Like what, for example?" I asked. His list made my jaw drop, with John Owen's *The Mortification of Sin* and J. I. Packer's *Evangelism and the Sovereignty of God* topping the list. For some, becoming a new creation could involve becoming literate.

Allen's impressive list of books came before conversion. Raised in a Christian home, he grew increasingly rebellious because of hypocrisy he saw in his Christian school. He read the Qur'an, the Book of Mormon, and a lot of "Eastern stuff." The rise of the new atheists—Richard Dawkins, Christopher Hitchens, and Sam Harris—provided the intellectual firepower he needed to reject the Christian faith with a vengeance. He especially loved Hitchens and read his regular column in *Vanity Fair* magazine. But reading Hitchens also turned him around. Like millions of Hitchens fans, Allen couldn't wait to get his hands on the new release *God Is Not Great: How Religion Poisons Everything.* "I really liked Hitchens. Read everything he put out, watched everything he put out on YouTube. He had this venom that really resonated with me. Not only are these [religious] people intellectually wrong, they're morally wrong."

But he found Hitchens to be inconsistent. Allen just didn't buy Hitchens's insistence that atheists could have a basis for morality apart from God. He liked how atheism gave him the intellectual foundation for immorality—hence, lots of drug use, sex, nihilistic music, and so on. "Hitchens claimed that morality is innate to the human experience, and we don't need to know where it comes from in order to abide by it—and that didn't make sense to me." That started an internal crisis, complete with "panic attacks and an inability to sleep." He only found relief after a one-on-one Bible study of the book of Romans. As he moved into his dorm on the first day on his college campus, he met Christians he first thought were "knuckle-dragging Baptists." For some odd reason, he accepted an invitation to study the Bible with one of them. Less than two months later, Allen became a Christian.

> If people need to . . . see the gospel lived
> out in a variety of ways, what better place
> for that to occur than in a local church?

In response to my final question in all my interviews, "What three factors were the most important in your conversion?" Allen said the contrast between sincere Christians at college and the hypocrites back home was number one. The book of Romans placed second. Then Allen told me that Hitchens's book was one of the three. I laughed and asked, for the sake of clarification, "So, an important person in your conversion was Christopher Hitchens?" Allen replied immediately, "Oh, yeah. And I wrote and told him that! You know, when people get converted, they want to go tell all their lost friends. Well, Christopher Hitchens was my lost friend. So I wrote him a letter, told him how much I appreciated his work, and that I became a Christian and he had started that process. I wanted to tell him, 'Man, you're so close.' But I never heard back from him."

The Voice of the Greatest Author

I also asked people, "How about the Bible? Was there a particular part of the Bible that you read that was significant?" Again a mixed response. Some gave the same answer I heard about other books: "Nah. Not really." But many did say that reading the Bible "shook me up," "really messed me up," "was so different than what I expected," or "was something I just couldn't put down." Jacob had read only a small part of the Bible until, while attending a student conference, he went to his hotel room and just read and read for more than three hours.

Shelly told me, "I cried every time I got to the end of the gospels and read about Jesus dying on the cross." She started crying right then—sitting in the midst of a crowded plaza in the center of her campus. She had never read any of the Bible until friends challenged her to give it a try. She started with a "well, why not" attitude but found herself overwhelmed with emotion when reading the closing chapters of Matthew, Mark, Luke, and John.

I asked her why those particular passages made her cry: "Can you tell me what was going on inside you at those points?" It took her a long time to compose herself. Out came the tissues. Finally, tearfully, she struggled to say, "He did it for me!" I asked her for one of her tissues.

The Role of Many in the Salvation of Individuals

Please note the importance of the church in evangelism. The concept of *body evangelism* can't be overstressed. If people need to hear multiple presentations from numerous voices and see the gospel lived out in a variety of ways, what better place for that to occur than in a local church?

One pastor told me he wants his congregation to embrace a "communal mission." Can't we see that in Paul's statement: "I planted the seed, Apollos watered it, but God has been making it grow" (1 Cor. 3:6)? We often apply Paul's teaching about the body of Christ and its members to discovering our spiritual gifts and employing them for the sake of the kingdom. And we must do so. But I urge us to also apply those verses to the specific kingdom work of evangelism. Granted, the primary sphere for using gifts is "for the common good" (12:7), which I take as the building up of the church. But drawing sharp lines between discipleship and evangelism has never served the church well.

Paul's teaching in 1 Corinthians 12–14 includes at least three core pillars: (1) the unity of the body, (2) the diversity of the parts of the body, and (3) the temptation to downplay certain parts of the body as "less honorable."

His statements about the first two points are brief and to the point: "There are different kinds of gifts, but the same Spirit distributes them. There are different kinds of service, but the same Lord" (1 Cor. 12:4–5). But then look at how much time he spends on the problem of undervaluing some members of the body. For over a dozen verses (12:12–26), he uses the illustrations of the foot and the hand, the ear and the eye, the eye and the hand, and the head and the feet. He warns of what can happen when we consider some parts as "weaker" or "less honorable" or "unpresentable."

C. S. Lewis's reflections about membership can serve us well here.

> The very word *membership* is of Christian origin, but it has been taken over by the world and emptied of all meaning. . . . It must be most emphatically stated that the items or particulars included in a homogeneous class are almost the reverse of what St. Paul meant by *members*. By *members* he meant what we should call *organs*, things essentially different from, and complementary to, one another. . . . I am afraid that when we describe a man as "a member of the Church" we usually mean nothing Pauline; we mean only that he is a unit.[1]

Some people "plant the seed"; they present the gospel message in full. Others "water that seed"; they answer questions, provide resources, suggest websites, and ask questions. And some find themselves drawn to extraordinary concentrated times of prayer for the lost. (Yes, we all should pray. But some have a distinct call for a unique ministry of intercession beyond the ordinary.) We are all members with distinct roles. We are not mere units with identical functions.

I see some evidence of this in the way John constructed his gospel. He tells us, quite clearly, that his many stories were "written that you may believe that Jesus is the Messiah, the Son of God, and that by believing you may have life in his name" (John 20:31). He could have told us many other stories (see John 21:25). But his evangelistic mission was better served through retelling of encounters between Jesus and several different people.

We meet Nicodemus, a religious intellectual who needed to hear theological arguments for his need for more than religion (John 3:1–21). We meet a Samaritan woman who needed water that could satisfy a deeper thirst than anything she could find in relationships with men (4:4–26). We witness an unforgettable episode of religious men shaming an adulterous woman. We learn that they all need saving grace—the men need to put down stones and the woman needs to go and leave her life of sin (8:1–11). We could point out many different facets of the gospel, displayed through the people in John's drama: people healed of diseases, both young (4:43–53) and old (5:5–9), crowds (6:1–14) and individuals (9:1–25), and on and on we could go. Just as my interviewees heard from a number of voices, John's gospel helps his readers do the same.

Jesus himself provides commentary on the ways different people play different roles in the harvest. After stating words we love to quote, "Open your eyes and look at the fields! They are ripe for harvest," he adds an often neglected nuance: "Even now the one who reaps draws a wage and harvests a crop for eternal life, so that the sower and the reaper may be glad together. Thus the saying 'One sows and another reaps' is true. I sent you to reap what you have not worked for. Others have done the hard work, and you have reaped the benefits of their labor" (John 4:35–38). Some sow. Some reap. Jesus values both.

> I wonder how much fun we'll have in heaven
> bumping into people who played parts
> in our conversion and reminiscing about
> the ways God wove our paths together.

I once saw a masterfully produced video about "the chain of evangelism." It showed one person sharing the gospel with a friend. That friend then went and told someone else. Then that third link in the chain extended to a fourth, and so on. I loved the video and have no complaints about it. But I wonder about a different kind of video that

I hope someone produces someday. Instead of the chain of evangelism, I'd like to see "the chorus of evangelists," dramatizing how one person's conversion came after hearing from many witnesses.

The video would follow one main character who heard something from her parents when she was young, something else from a friend at school, saw acts of gospel-shaped kindnesses along the way, heard an intellectually rigorous defense of the Bible's authority during her freshman year in college, and so on.

I wonder how much fun we'll have in heaven bumping into people who played parts in our conversion and reminiscing about the ways God wove our paths together. I'm looking forward to seeing one particular guy who handed me a "Jesus magazine" (they were popular during the 1970s) while I pumped gas into his car. (That was also common during the 1970s.)

I kept looking at the pile of Christian literature on the back seat in his car. He guessed I was open to spiritual things and thought it worth the effort to give me something to read. He never said a word, and I never saw his face. He just handed me the magazine along with the money for his gas. Maybe in heaven I'll recognize him by his arm!

Challenging Common Clichés

Having observed that people tend to come to faith gradually and communally, it's worth reflecting on the theological underpinnings behind those gradual, communal conversions. Part of that reflecting process involves examining some clichés we sometimes use about evangelism. We need to think clearly, deeply, and biblically about how we express ourselves. Here are a few examples:

"People belong before they believe."
I appreciate the sentiment behind this statement, and I agree that people often identify with a church or Christian fellowship before they cross from unbelief to belief. But we need to be careful not to push this too far. There's a world of difference between identifying with a group of Christians and belonging to Christ. Let's not blur the line between being objects of God's wrath and being saved from

that wrath. If we do, we'll distort the urgent nature of the gospel's demands for repentance and faith. Some people even advocate having nonbelievers serve in our churches in upfront or public ways. They insist that people don't need to be Christians to hand out bulletins or sing in the choir. I would caution against this and urge careful thinking about church membership and what "belonging" really means.

"Leading people to the Lord."

Sometimes this is expressed as a question: "How many people have you personally led to the Lord?" This fails to see the conversion process as divinely orchestrated; instead, it gives credit to the person who just happened to be at the end of a long sequence of people God placed along the path. It also reinforces some prideful attitudes that distort a biblical understanding of how God uses people in his miraculous saving work. I think it's better to talk about "seeing people come to faith" or "watching God work in people's lives" or similar phrases that point the spotlight on God and away from ourselves.

"You can't argue people into the kingdom."

Again, I appreciate the concern behind these words. We need to practice "gentleness and respect" (1 Peter 3:15) as we proclaim the gospel. Talking about God's saving love with a scowl on our face or anger in our voice sure seems like shooting ourselves in the foot.

Part of the problem, I think, stems from the usual connotations of the word *argue*. People often tell me they want to be careful "not to cram Jesus down anyone's throat" or "bash someone over the head with a Bible." (The visual images dazzle, don't they?) I firmly agree: avoid cramming and bashing at all costs! But I fear people sometimes mean that *any* kind of rational persuasion or intellectual engagement has no place in evangelism. They drive a wedge between the intellectual and the spiritual. But the stories I heard wove together interactions with people and the arguments they made.

When people tell me, "No one has ever been argued into the kingdom," I want to respond:

- Why not?
- How do you know?
- I think I was argued into the kingdom.
- I know many people who say arguments played a big role in their conversion.
- One friend told me, "I read my way to faith." He read lots of apologetics books with lots of arguments in them.

The more important response about the role of argument in evangelism comes from Scripture. Jesus modeled engaging conversations with outsiders. (Remember Nicodemus.) Paul appealed to logic and argument in his preaching. (Remember Mars Hill.) We're told to be ready with answers. (Remember 1 Peter 3:15.) And the very fact that God inspired a book full of words, constructed with arguments, and laced with logic should point us in the direction of seeing people as integrated, whole persons with an intellect, affections, volition, and social connections—woven together rather than compartmentalized. We'll consider this further in the next chapter.

Some Practical Implications for Body Evangelism

If people tend to come to faith by hearing from an array of people, how can we best equip Christians for evangelism? I'll offer three ideas here and share more ideas in the second half of this book.

> Training in evangelism and apologetics
> is for all God's people, not just those
> with the gift of evangelism.

First, training in evangelism and apologetics is for all God's people, not just those with the gift of evangelism. Part of the church's discipleship mission is equipping her people to "always be prepared" (1 Peter 3:15). Nonevangelists will sound different (and probably feel different) from the Billy Grahams or Ravi Zachariases in our congregations. But they play indispensable roles, even if they feel weaker (see 1 Cor. 12:22). In fact, sometimes those who seem less polished or professional come across with more credibility.

Second, we must provide evangelism and apologetics training hand in hand with teaching about spiritual gifts. When we provide teaching about what it means to join our churches (what we believe, how we do things, why we structure church life the way we do, and so forth), we should also help people discover their spiritual gift or gifts and explore ways that they may fit into the body of Christ. Remember, as C. S. Lewis pointed out, we're *members*, not just units.

Third, we need to make it relatively easy (nothing is really easy when it comes to evangelism) and normal for Christians to invite outsiders to church. Our websites should be outsider-friendly, and our people need ready-made invitations (both hard-copy and electronic) to give or send to friends. But let's face it: for some people, coming to a worship service is not the first step. (If your Muslim friend invited you to his mosque, would you say, "Sure. Sounds fun!"?) Churches need numerous "entry-level" events that are less threatening than a formal worship service—Bible studies in homes, discussions in coffee shops, or social events where Christians and non-Christians get to know each other over time.

Conclusion

When my sons were young, they played basketball in a community league. Using a draft system that rated all the players, the teams turned out remarkably even in their level of skill. Each team had one or two superstars who were drafted in the first two rounds, three or four solid players with moderate skills, and one or two players who joined the league because their parents thought they should be "well rounded." Since the league required all the players to play an equal number of minutes, every coach had the challenge of making their mix of players work well as a team. You couldn't just rely on the superstars to carry the day. Everyone had their role to play and had to perform to the best of their ability. Teams that won championships did so not because of one or two all-stars but because everyone fulfilled their roles.

My boys had the good fortune of having a great coach who led them to several championship seasons. I studied his approach carefully as he spent more time with the lower-level players than with the leaders. On one team, one boy, I'll call him Eddie, went the entire season without scoring a single basket. His skill level, to put it mildly, needed remedial help. The coach worked with him extensively on how to make a layup. He broke it down to its component parts: get in position, take one purposeful short step toward the side of the basket, bounce the ball off the backboard, follow through after you release the ball, and so forth. Week after week at practice, Eddie worked on layups. He made only a small percentage of them. But he never gave up.

Then in the final thirty seconds of the championship game, our team tied the score with a long jumper from one of the superstars. The other team hurriedly took the ball out of bounds and tried to advance it for a fast break. If they caught us off guard, they could score the winning basket with no time left on the clock. Instead, they failed to see Eddie lurking in the back court (perhaps because he was too slow to sprint to the other end of the court). Their in-bounds pass went right into Eddie's hands, standing right near our basket—at the very spot where he had practiced layups week after week. You guessed it: he made the layup! His very first basket of the season was *the* winning basket of the championship game. Too bad this was long before the world of cell phone video cameras. That shot would have gone viral!

We need to see evangelism as a team sport. Our "team" will have our superstars—pastors who preach powerful sermons, evangelists who make dramatic presentations, and apologists who win debates. We'll also have middle-level players who invite people to church, start gospel conversations, and lead evangelistic Bible studies. But let's not ignore (or fail to equip) the "weaker" teammates who might attach a link to an evangelistic video on their Facebook page or retweet a quote from their pastor's sermon or, after much practice and with great trepidation, say to a friend, "Would you ever like to come to church with me?"

BRAINSTORMS: INVITATIONS

Inviting people to a social gathering of believers or a Bible study or a worship service or any kind of pre-evangelistic event seems more intimidating than it should be. We feel more awkward doing the asking than many non-Christians feel about being asked. But choose wisely. For some people, a worship service would be too much of a leap. A simple invitation to a meal together might be the better start. A social gathering of Christians could work as the next step. But you don't have to have the whole scheme mapped out ahead of time.

Here are a few ways to start the process.

- We'd love to have you guys over for dinner sometime. Could that work with your schedules?
- We're having a cookout next Saturday. It'll be a whole mix of people—some from where I work, some from the neighborhood, some from my church. Can you join us?
- I wonder if you'd ever be interested in joining me at a Bible study I go to.
- Some friends of mine and I get together and discuss spiritual things on Sunday nights. Would you ever like to join us?
- I don't know if you're looking for a church to go to on Easter. Are you? If you'd want to come, just let me know.

CHAPTER 3

Variously

A my felt exhausted. Understandably so. Her high school guid-
ance counselor told her she would need "a lot of extracurricular
activities" on her college application to get accepted anywhere. So
she joined the swim team, the cheerleading squad, the chess club,
the yearbook committee, and several other clubs to impress a variety
of admissions offices. And it worked! She got accepted to her first-
choice college.

At some point during her first semester, she thought she should
probably join a lot of extracurricular activities so she'd have a great
resume when applying for jobs after college. So she joined lots of
preprofessional associations as well as a sorority, the women's flag
football team, and other clubs to fill her schedule to the brim. "All of
a sudden I was just overwhelmed and realized I didn't want the rest
of my life to be just like high school. Jobs, leadership, having authority, respect from others . . . [those things] weren't what satisfied me
or made me happy. I was just so overwhelmed."

> There was great diversity in what
> motivated others to move forward in
> the journey from unbelief to faith.

Sometime during that first year, a friend invited her to a Christian organization's weekly meeting. Thinking that *too* would look
good on a resume, she went. I asked if she liked the meeting. She

shrugged her shoulders. I asked what she remembered. She indicated, "not much." "Did somebody speak?" I asked. She couldn't remember who or about what. What she did remember was that someone (not the main speaker) quoted something from the Bible: "Come to me, all you who are weary and burdened, and I will give you rest." It was Matthew 11:28, but that didn't matter to her at the time. What caught her attention was, "Finding your rest in God—that hit me because that's what I was looking for. That was a biggie!" Curious how Jesus might have something to do with "rest," she signed up for a Bible study and started regular meetings with an older Christian student. Less than two months later, she became a Christian.

Multifaceted People

What struck me about Amy's story was how it differed from all the others. She linked to the gospel through the hinge of "rest." No one else said that. But there was great diversity in what motivated others to move forward in the journey from unbelief to faith. Several talked about the need for forgiveness of sins. But not as many as you might expect.

Rebecca told me she needed cleansing from the damage caused by sin. That's slightly different from the need for forgiveness from committing sins. Of course, she did acknowledge her need for forgiveness in the classic sense of how we think about the gospel. But that's not how she began her description of her experience. Andrew spoke of how coming to faith "lifted a burden" caused by a sinful lifestyle. Alyssa described something different than a cleansing. For her, it was more of a "total makeover" that removed a kind of shame.

Several people told how a sense of belonging dominated their story. They found a new community that felt so different than their network of shallow friendships or the dysfunction of their family. For Jack, it was a sense of cohesion; the gospel helped him make sense of all of life. Nathaniel described a relief from lifelong anger that started when he heard how Jesus's death satisfied both God's holy anger and infinite love for him. And Miles told me how thrilled he was when he realized God was an authority worth following.

For some, intellectual answers paved the route to the gospel. For others, emotions dominated the story. I had one fascinating conversation with a married couple, Gary and Maureen, whose stories contrasted dramatically. His involved logic; hers was drenched in tears. He read books in a library; she wept through worship songs at a church. He devoured internet articles on apologetics; she couldn't believe God could love her with all her sin and shame.

And quite a few people told me of several differing factors that played a part in their stories. They wove together intellect, emotions, social connections, and other factors in a balanced way. At the end of all my interviews, I asked people to sum up their narratives by identifying the three most significant parts of their journey. I started making elaborate color-coded charts to display the rainbow of suggestions—intellectual questions indicated as green, emotional struggles coded as blue, relational connections shaded as pink, and so forth. Here's my point: no single list was monochromatic.

Along these lines, we have much to learn from Christian philosopher Clifford Williams. He states his view of conversion this way: "Most people of faith acquire their faith partly because they feel that it meets . . . existential needs and partly because they think it makes sense or is true."[1] For Williams, coming to faith involves both "need and reason, an interplay that cannot be neatly demarcated." And he warns, "Theorists may have a clear-cut distinction in mind, but when we look at how people actually come to faith, the distinction gets blurred."[2]

Some of the "existential needs" he lists can be expressed like this:[3]

- "I need to feel that life ultimately makes sense."
- "I need to anticipate some kind of life after this earthly experience ends."
- "Even though this life has many disappointments, I need to rely on the possibility of a place after this life—one without disappointments or pain or evil or sadness."
- "I need to trust that there is such a thing as goodness and beauty and purity."

- "I need to love and be loved. And those emotions are not just illusions."
- "I crave meaning—not just in temporary ways but in ways that last forever."

The great news for us is that the gospel satisfies those and many other needs while also answering many rational questions.

Our Multifaceted Message

We need to see connections between the diversity of faith experiences and the richness of the gospel. We have a multifaceted message that connects with complex people in a variety of ways. Do you resist this? Do you fear I might lose the centrality of the atonement in all this? I understand your caution. I fear the same danger. And church history is littered with times when people replaced the atonement with other things and, in the process, lost the gospel. As J. I. Packer observes, "Throughout my sixty-three years as an evangelical believer, the penal substitutionary understanding of the cross of Christ has been a flashpoint of controversy and division among Protestants."[4]

Hoping not to diminish the centrality of substitutionary atonement, I want us to also consider some of the many words the New Testament uses to proclaim, explain, or unpack the implications of that substitutionary atonement—propitiation, justification, salvation, rebirth, regeneration, redemption, reconciliation, and sanctification.

If the Bible itself employs various terms to highlight different aspects of our gospel message, we shouldn't be gun-shy to do likewise. For some of our hearers, the judicial image of propitiation will resonate. For others, the economic concept of redemption will make more sense. Still others will have the light bulb turn on through the courtroom vocabulary of justification. And another crowd may be reached best through familial, relational terms like reconciliation or adoption.[5]

We might also try a variety of ways to talk about God and see which connects in the most compelling ways. The Bible refers to God as a father, a husband, a judge, a king, a priest, and quite a few other roles. Some people are longing to hear of a father who pursues. Still others hunger for a husband who reconciles. Others want to find a judge who pardons. Why stick with just one image or title or dimension if God has chosen to reveal himself in numerous, diverse ways.[6]

The diversity and richness of the New Testament's discussions of the gospel allow for and, indeed, demand diversity in evangelistic strategies. This is why we see a variety of approaches to preaching for conversion modeled in the New Testament itself. Don Carson lists eight such motivations: fear of judgment, the burden of guilt, shame, the need for future grace, the attractiveness of truth, a general despairing sense of need, response to grace and love, and a desire to be on the side of what is right.[7] He concludes, "We do not have the right to choose only one of these motivations in people and to appeal to it restrictively."[8]

Thus, we must tell people of their objective guilt before a righteous God. In fact, this must maintain its central place as the nonnegotiable heart of our message. But our starting point for evangelistic discussions can begin in a variety of places. We see a classic example of this in Mark 2:1–12 where a man is brought to Jesus for physical healing (which Jesus *does* address!) but soon finds he has a greater need for forgiveness.

We can proclaim our multifaceted gospel to multifaceted people by using a variety of analogies. Readers of *Mere Christianity* see the many illustrations and analogies C. S. Lewis paraded out to try to connect with diverse people with diverse images. Michael Ward offers what he calls a "brief survey" of Lewis's images of conversion:

> Becoming a Christian (passing from death to life) is like joining in a campaign of sabotage, like falling at someone's feet or putting yourself in someone's hands, like taking on board fuel or food, like laying down your rebel arms and surrendering, saying sorry, laying yourself open, turning full speed astern; it is like killing part of yourself, like learning to walk or to write, like buying God a present with his own money; it is like a drowning man clutching at a

rescuer's hand, like a tin soldier or a statue becoming alive, like waking after a long sleep, like getting close to someone or becoming infected, like dressing up or pretending or playing; it is like emerging from the womb or hatching from an egg; it is like a compass needle swinging to north, or a cottage being made into a palace, or a field being plowed and resown, or a horse turning into a Pegasus, or a greenhouse roof becoming bright in the sunlight; it is like coming around from anesthetic, like coming in out of the wind, like going home.[9]

Does all this overwhelm you? I hope it does just the opposite. A deep appreciation for the richness of the gospel can liberate us from presenting the gospel in just one way. It can expand our effectiveness and broaden the scope of our outreach. It can also reach deeper to aches that throb far below the surface. Then the gospel can penetrate in ways we might not have expected or even known about.

> The gospel can touch people on many
> levels. It can help make sense of our
> world better than other worldviews.

I have found help in expressing this from a new vocabulary term: *capaciousness*. At least, it was new to me when I first read it in Alister McGrath's excellent book *Mere Apologetics: How to Help Seekers and Skeptics Find Faith*. Merriam-Webster defines *capacious* as "containing or capable of containing a great deal."[10] You can see the idea of "capacity" in the word. McGrath says, "Apologetics is grounded in a deep appreciation of the intellectual capaciousness and spiritual richness of the Christian faith."[11] And, "The intellectual capaciousness of the Christian faith is one of its greatest strengths, and it has considerable apologetic potential."[12]

I would go further. Not only does the gospel have "intellectual capaciousness," it also has emotional and existential capaciousness. In other words, the gospel can touch people on many levels. It can help make sense of our world better than other worldviews. It can also satisfy deep longings and relieve deep-seated pain.

Yet another way to consider the richness of the gospel and its relation to people's holistic nature can be seen through the word *shalom*. Far more than meaning peace or a mere absence of hostility, this important Hebrew term implies "completion and fulfillment— of entering into a state of wholeness and unity, a restored relationship."[13] A form of the word is even used to describe the whole (i.e., uncut) stones for the altar (Deut. 27:6; Josh. 8:31) and also of the dressed stones used for the temple (1 Kings 6:7).[14] When Paul wrote, "Since we have been justified through faith, we have peace with God" (Rom. 5:1), he had a fuller picture in mind than mere positional truth.

We need to reflect often, deeply, and comprehensively on the gospel so we see and appreciate its capaciousness. Then we'll be able to converse with people about a very wide range of topics and see the links to God's good news. To quote Clifford Williams again, "A rich and lively faith cannot consist simply of intellectual assent. It has to have the emotional depth that Christian virtues such as love, joy, peace, patience and kindness possess."[15] Hopefully people may someday say about us what Owen Barfield once said about his friend C. S. Lewis: "Somehow what he thought about everything was secretly present in what he said about anything."[16]

Our Multifaceted Neighbors

The unsaved people God places around us need the new life offered by the cross. We may not see the underlying dramas, but we can trust God's power to penetrate their facades of satisfaction and self-reliance. Our capacious gospel can bring wholeness and shalom to people on numerous levels—even if we can't see all their dramas when we evangelize. For our hearers, our good news may be even better than we think.

Consider examples from the lives of two well-known people:

Christopher Hitchens and Michael Richards. We've already considered Hitchens's intellectual prowess and the limits thereof in the
previous chapter. What many people don't know involves the pain
lurking behind his many intellectual tirades. I've always marveled
at Hitchens's brilliant writing and fluid style of expressing complex
issues. I wept as I read his book *Mortality*, in which he described his
battle with and ultimate succumbing to esophageal cancer. As only
Christopher could, he maintained a sense of humor as he approached
the end of his life with quips like "The thing about Stage Four [can-
cer] is that there is no such thing as Stage Five."[17]

Years before, I remember hearing him respond to an NPR inter-
viewer regarding his personal memoir, *Hitch 22*. When asked why his
mother played such a prominent role in his book, Hitchens replied:

> My father was, as you say, a lifelong Navy man, so I had
> this rather morose Tory in my background who was hit off
> brilliantly, by contrast, by my mother, who I always called
> Yvonne. And I call her Yvonne in my chapter, because it's a
> stylish name and because she was a stylish girl.
>
> And her story's a tragic one and it ended tragically, in that
> having waited I think rather too long, because divorce and
> separation were extremely frowned upon in that set in those
> days. She did take up with another man after my brother
> and I had grown up, and it didn't quite work out. In fact, it
> didn't work out at all. And they made a decision to put an
> end to their lives and committed suicide together in Athens.
>
> I think I had a chance to save her and failed to grasp it.
> She tried to call me from Athens and failed. Though I might
> have just missed the call by a few minutes, I don't know. But
> I've always been certain that if she'd heard my voice, she
> wouldn't have done it. So I've been trying to write my way
> out of that ever since.[18]

You don't need a degree in psychology to grasp how deep that
pain dug into Hitchens's life. Perhaps that's why he drank so much

alcohol. He needed a salvation more effective than "trying to write his way out of that." The gospel is capacious enough to lift a burden that heavy.

Michael Richards also needs the capacious gospel to help him with his guilt. Most people know Richards as Kramer from the television sitcom *Seinfeld*. A brilliant physical comic, Richards returned to comedy clubs after *Seinfeld*'s eight-year television run ended. He probably would have found immense success in the stand-up world, given his level of fame. But one fateful night he responded to an African American man in the crowd with a slew of ethnic slurs. An arsenal of cell phone cameras caught it, and the video went viral. Richards's racism destroyed his career and harmed him far beyond the stage.

If you can handle it, you might be able to find the video of the comedian's racial tirade online, along with several appearances on late-night television shows where Richards tried to apologize profusely. But the sincerity of his contrition never opened up doors for more comedy gigs. As best as I can tell, he still hasn't found absolution.

Seven years later, as he and Jerry Seinfeld conversed on the internet program *Comedians in Cars Getting Coffee*, they broached the painful subject of Michael's meltdown on stage.[19]

"I busted up," Richards told his obviously concerned and compassionate friend. "It broke me down." He confessed it as inexcusable. "It was a selfish response. . . . I should have been working selflessly." He even told how he tried to escape by taking a solitary vacation to Bali—about as far away from the comedy club as he could run. He thanked Jerry for "sticking by me" but admitted, "Inside, it still kicks me around."

If you watch the episode, it's hard not to notice the pain on Richards's face and the equally intense concern on Seinfeld's. Trying to offer pardon, Jerry said, "Well, that's up to you. If I were you, I'd tell myself, 'I've been carrying this long enough. I'm gonna put it down now.'" As the camera zoomed in on Richards, he softly replied, "Yeah. Yeah." But I wasn't convinced he'd found the atonement he needed. Despite the pronouncement from the high priest of comedy, Jerry Seinfeld, Michael Richards's sin needed more than just the self-effort of letting go of a burden. We all need the once-for-all finished sacrifice of the Messiah and all its capaciousness.

One Very Complex Issue

In my interviews, I never asked anything about sex. But the topic came up almost every time. Whether we like it or not, evangelizing in the twenty-first century will involve discussions of sexuality. We should prepare ourselves accordingly. As Russell Moore has said, we minister today to "refugees from the sexual revolution."[20]

> Evangelizing in our sexually promiscuous world today requires sensitivity to the scars people bear . . . and the questions they can't imagine being answered from the Bible.

God designed sex to connect people in powerful, all-encompassing ways. That's why the Bible describes the experience as "becom[ing] one flesh" (Gen. 2:24). Violating God's design for sex damages people in profound ways. Adultery adulterates. Within its God-designed parameters, sex unites, forges security, and builds trust. Outside that limited scope, sexual sin disintegrates, causes pain, and builds walls. That may be part of why Paul warns, "All other sins a person commits are outside the body, but whoever sins sexually, sins against their own body" (1 Cor. 6:18).

Evangelizing in our sexually promiscuous world today requires sensitivity to the scars people bear, the anger some feel, the puzzles they can't unravel, and the questions they can't imagine being answered from the Bible. We need numerous approaches depending on the range of starting points. Some people mock us for our antiquated views. Some ache from sexual abuse. Some can't quite put their finger on it, but they know something is out of whack.

Donna Freitas, a research associate at several academic institutions, has studied college students' experiences with sex for many years. The subtitle of her book *The End of Sex* declares, "The Hookup Culture Is Leaving a Generation Unhappy, Sexually Unfulfilled, and Confused About Intimacy."[21] She begins her disturbing book with, "Amid the seemingly endless partying on America's college campuses lies a thick layer of melancholy, insecurity, and isolation that no one can seem to shake."[22]

Freitas does not claim to be a Christian, but her interpretations of her research findings echo biblical principles. God designed sex to promote intimacy. Rejecting his plan leads to isolation and worse. While some laud the current sexual "liberation" for women to control their own bodies, Freitas points out, "It is true that . . . hookup culture allows women to put off relationships. Yet it doesn't simply *allow* this, it fairly *forbids* the formation of long-term romantic attachments, something both genders complain about in private."[23]

The students I interviewed gave voice to the findings of Freitas and other researchers. They spoke of having sex because it was the norm, the expected, and the demand of a culture that mocks virginity. Some spoke with no emotion on their face at all. But many looked pained as they told me, "I wanted to say no to having sex, but I couldn't figure out how to say it," or "I wondered what was wrong with me that I didn't just want to have sex with as many guys as I could." No one told them why that might lead to a life of regret.

Some didn't necessarily feel guilty about having a lot of sex with a lot of partners. But they did express disappointment, loneliness, alienation, or severe depression. And they made the connections between sex and their emotional struggles. Trudy offered an impressive evaluation of her sexual promiscuity: "I think with my parents' divorce I also had a lot of 'father hunger,' and so I looked to guys to fulfill me. I just wanted someone to like me for who I was, and so it was easy for me to turn to guys for what I thought was affection." This may seem obvious. But consider what else she told me: "When my parents got divorced, I figured that love doesn't exist. If love doesn't exist, then God doesn't exist."

Interestingly, it was the failure of yet another sexual relationship that played a part in Trudy's encounter with the gospel. Her father hunger drove her to have a boyfriend move in with her, but his abusive ways led to her kicking him out. Just a few nights of being alone led to a profound loneliness. So when some coworkers invited her to a Bible study, she went—not because she was interested in God (remember, she had concluded that God *couldn't* exist, not just that he *didn't* exist), but because she thought, "OK, I'll go to your Bible study because if I don't, I'm just going to go home to an empty apartment. And I'd rather hang out with religious people than be alone."

Do you see why I say this is a complex issue that presents complex challenges for us? I hope you also see the wonderful opportunities this mess creates. People have rejected the very plan that could have saved them the pain, anger, abuse, guilt, shame, and regret that come from marriage-less sex. But God's plan involves more than rules for conduct or strategies for living. It also includes forgiveness, washing, rebirth, and the power to be made a new creation. The Lawgiver is also the Redeemer. The demander of payment for sin is also the provider of payment for sin. He is both just and the justifier.

Thus, the emotional dynamics of evangelism in a sex-charged culture call for theological depth, communication excellence, and interpersonal dexterity. We should anticipate hostility from some who love darkness. We should not be surprised by mockery and ridicule from a culture that has invested a lot in sexual "liberation." But we can assume a fair amount of pain behind the taunts, jokes, and attacks.

At the same time, we need to respond with a blend of compassion, conviction, and clarity. And we can find great encouragement that despite the power of sexual sin, God's power to save is greater. As Mary Eberstadt triumphantly declares, "The truth that has not been reckoned with by religion's cultured despisers today is this: Christianity is being built more and more by these very witnesses—by people who have come to embrace the difficult and longstanding Christian rulebook not because they know nothing of the [sexual] revolution and its fallout, but because they know all too much."[24]

A Multifaceted Strategy

Fortunately, the gospel can be expressed in a variety of ways to meet a variety of people. As mentioned above, the fact that Jesus spoke differently to different people provides a basis for a variety of approaches. The same could be shown from Paul's variety of approaches and messages.

Tim Keller speaks of preaching "the gospel in all its forms" and observes, "There must be one gospel, yet there are clearly different forms in which that one gospel can be expressed. This is the Bible's own way of speaking of the gospel and we should stick with it."[25] Most often the gospel focuses on a person's need for forgiveness; other times, the gospel shines the light on the advances of God's kingdom. But each approach is just an aspect of the gospel in its completeness, and they complement one another. We dare not pit a "gospel of atonement" against a "gospel of the kingdom" as some want to do.

Keller offers specific suggestions for how we can proclaim our rich gospel to our spiritually impoverished neighbors. Although he wrote primarily for pastors as they prepared sermons, his ideas have applicability for all Christians as they engage in conversations with unsaved friends, family, and acquaintances.

Here are my summations of just some of Keller's suggestions:

1. Don't try to put every point of the gospel in every presentation.
2. Adapt your gospel presentation to your hearers. For those with a religious background, stress the uniqueness of the gospel's grace for individual sinners. For those of a postmodern, relativistic perspective, show how the gospel provides what we're all looking for but not finding in relationships or personal autonomy.
3. Balance discussions of the individual-eternal-life gospel and the kingdom-gospel. Point people in both directions—inward and outward. The gospel is good news in both ways.

As mentioned above, the gospel can be expressed in a variety of ways because the kingdom of God has the same quality. Consider all the many parables Jesus told in Matthew 13 to help people realize how great a concept the kingdom is. He likened the kingdom to seeds sown on different kinds of soils; to weeds and wheat; to a mustard seed; to yeast, treasure hidden in a field, a pearl of great value, and to a net that catches all kinds of fish.

Just think about the variety of images in that list. And try to sense the variety of appeals made by them. The first two parables help us understand things about the kingdom that might contrast with our preconceived ideas about it. The mustard seed and yeast parables encourage us to keep the long-term view in sight. The parables of the treasure and the pearl appeal to our affections to long for the kingdom as far more than an explanatory concept. And the net parable starts out exciting but finishes with a harsh ending. We could probably ascribe other attributes to these parables, but the point is that they touch us in a variety of ways. They don't just inform; they engage. Parables don't just give timelines or explanations; they stimulate longings and trigger imaginations.

You get the idea that Jesus could have kept going with parable after parable and still not have covered the topic exhaustively. In fact, I think he implies just that when, after sharing the parable of the soils, a lamp, and a growing seed in Mark 4, he pauses to reflect, "What shall we say the kingdom of God is like, or what parable shall we use to describe it?" (v. 30). At first we might wonder, "What do you mean, 'What parable shall we use?' You just told three good ones!" And we certainly can't assume Jesus was stumped or confused. His rhetorical question, "What shall we say the kingdom of God is like?" should lead us to the conclusion that no single parable can capture all we should know, feel, and desire about the kingdom.

We can frame our multifaceted strategy under a number of rubrics. We proclaim good news that has the potential to set captives free, open blind eyes, soften hardened hearts, and bring outsiders in. We can also help people escape the slavery of "casting off restraint" and liberate them to find blessing in keeping God's law. Does that sound counterintuitive? Consider Proverbs 29:18: "Where there is no revelation, the people cast off restraint; but blessed is he who keeps the law" (NIV 1984).[26]

Often mistranslated as "Where there is no vision, the people perish" (with little or no mention of the second half of the verse), this proverb talks about *God's* revealing of his truth, not *our* setting organizational goals or writing personal mission statements. The proverb tells us how wonderful it is that God "is there and he is not silent."[27] We are not left to grope around in the dark for answers or, worse, look to find our moral compass within ourselves. God has given us his law, statutes, and ordinances (isn't it amazing how many terms are used in Psalm 19!) so we can build our lives on his blueprint.

And if we do, we can be "blessed." That word is packed with dimensions—and they're all good. To be blessed is to find approval from God, to experience deep happiness and contentment, and to have a firm foundation to all aspects of our lives.

> When we proclaim the gospel in all its fullness, with all its dimensions, we bring a multifaceted salvation to multifaceted people.

I began this chapter with Amy's story of coming to faith. It revolved around rest. Her many activities wore her out, and the gospel's promise of rest drew her in. But I wondered if a deeper fatigue lurked behind her schedule's fullness. As our conversation wound down, after I closed my notebook and turned off my recorder, I mentioned that I noticed she spoke of her mother several times. "What about your father?" I wondered. "How did he respond to your newfound faith?"

She answered more quietly and with less eye contact than the entire rest of our time together. She told me she didn't really know her father all that much. He left the family when she was ten years old. He doesn't contact her often. In fact, she hadn't heard from him in several years.

Her tiredness came from a deeper exhaustion than from too many extracurricular activities. The people we meet, speak with, preach to, and listen to have deeper needs and a wider variety of aches than we can imagine. But the gospel is really good news for really bad situations. When we proclaim the gospel in all its fullness, with all its dimensions, we bring a multifaceted salvation to multifaceted people. We introduce them to the One who offers forgiveness, cleansing, purpose, meaning, freedom, a new identity, and, for some—best of all—rest.

BRAINSTORMS: COMMON GROUND

Some people who might not want to discuss spiritual issues are more than willing to banter about politics, sports, movies, books, and an almost endless list of other topics. Listening for the things that dominate their attention could suggest good places to engage about weightier issues. Perhaps some of these transitions to the gospel would be worth a try:

- That movie really raises some big issues, doesn't it? What did you think about the way they approached those topics?
- Isn't it amazing how, sometimes, a sunset or something beautiful makes you stop and wonder? Do you know what I mean?
- Are you much of a reader? What kinds of books do you like to read? What kinds of themes are you drawn to?
- How was your vacation? I'd love to hear about it. I always find that time away gives me space to think about things more deeply. Does that ever happen for you?

CHAPTER 4

Supernaturally

The most astonishing statement I heard in over forty hours of interviews was, "And so I decided to bring my Bible."

Erika grew up in a home with no religion other than the antagonism her atheist father occasionally expressed toward his own father, who had served as a pastor for more than fifty years. The way Erika worded it sounded harsh: "My family definitely doesn't have a religious backbone." She elaborated, "My family doesn't go to church. That's just never been part of my upbringing." When she went off to college, she never thought about religion or faith or God. She identified as an atheist who thought, "Just what you see here on earth—that's all there is." She filled her freshman year of college with the typical parties, boys, and alcohol without harming her grades. She came into college with a strong social resume. "I was my high school's golden girl—perfect GPA, star athlete, homecoming crown court, the whole bit." In college, "I had friends. I had things to fill my time with. I played lots of sports, lots of clubs; there was never that clear, vacant void." She felt no need for anything beyond her very full life.

When she came home after her first year, her parents announced plans to take a family vacation in Paris for the summer. "That's like a long summer to be just with your family . . . and so I decided to bring my Bible."

I had to interrupt her. "You had a Bible?"

"Yeah. I was given a Bible as a gift from a good friend of mine."

"How long ago?"

She shrugged her shoulders as if to express she didn't know and also confirm that her action was weird. In fact, she used the word *weird* several times when she told me about her decision to bring the Bible. It came "out of the blue." She even commented that it was one of those "really fat Bibles" that took up a lot of room in her suitcase—a rather small suitcase her father insisted she use because of airline restrictions. "I know. It's weird, right?" she added.

And she read that fat Bible. Every day! She read Matthew and Mark and several other parts of the New Testament. But "nothing really resonated with me. I don't remember anything I read over there." When she returned to college for her sophomore year, one of the first things she did was seek out a meeting of a Christian fellowship. She knew someone on her dorm floor who attended such a group. So she asked to join her.

I asked, "Did she invite you?"

"No," she told me emphatically. "I said [to her], 'Can I come?' So it was just weird."

The speaker that night presented a standard apologetics message about reasons why people should believe the Bible—archeological evidence, number of manuscripts, the historicity of the resurrection, and so forth. That event occurred over a year before my conversation with Erika, but she recounted specifics without hesitation. She remembered many points and supporting evidence—including an argument I've never heard included in an evangelistic presentation: when people stub their toe in a locker room, they call out Jesus's name as a curse word. "Why would you just say some random person's name that had no influence in the world" unless he really was more than just a random person? At that moment during the talk, she thought, "Oh no. I need to think about this." So she went back to her dorm room, found the speaker on Facebook, and "stalked" him. (Her word, not mine.) He wisely arranged for her to meet Catherine, a woman on his organization's staff team. They began to meet weekly.

"I kept drilling her with questions." For two months! Their conversations explored many intellectual questions—about the Bible's reliability, the historical fact of the resurrection, and the like. But Erika told me of another underlying drama.

"I didn't want to address truth. I carry a lot of pride, and so going for so long and just denying all possibility [of God's existence] and then having to turn around and be, like, 'Oh, you guys might actually be right . . .'"

But she kept meeting with Catherine, who wove together evidential apologetics and her own personal testimony. What I found interesting is that Erika really didn't relate to Catherine's story of faith. Hers involved a lot of pain and insecurity, while Erika's life was filled with success. "Our lives just didn't really line up. She struggled with some aspects of her life that I don't have a lot of trouble with."

And she didn't really understand why she kept meeting with Catherine. "I really just wanted to continue living life the way that I cut it out to be. That [religion or God] just wasn't the plan. I definitely struggled a lot with this idea of not having control over my life." Catherine spoke of "turning your life over to God" and letting him take control. "I had a lot of 'but what ifs.' Trusting someone else with my life was a big part" of Erika's discussions with Catherine. "But she was so patient with me."

You might think that an atheist, once taking the first step of acknowledging the existence of God, would then move incrementally to Christianity. You might expect a series of hurdles over major obstacles between "There is no god" and "Jesus is God, the Savior who atoned for sins, the Messiah who rose again, and the One I now bow before as my Lord." In fact, you may have even read somewhere that "people tend to come to faith gradually."

But for Erika, "Once I wrapped my head around the idea that there even could be a God, things moved a lot faster in my mind and heart. For me, once I decided for myself that I believed there was a God, personally, it was a very small step to believe that Jesus was God on earth. There were not a lot of 'If A then B, if B then C.'" She met with Catherine and said, "I'm ready to start following Jesus." And Catherine made sure she knew what she was doing, knew what "following Jesus" meant, and spent a fair amount of time talking about the sacrificial death of that same Jesus.

Erika wasn't the only one to use words like *weird*. I also heard the word *coincidence* a lot. People remembered "just happening" to be at a certain place at a certain time so they'd hear the gospel. Some spoke of "randomly" seeing an advertisement for a Christian event, or "stumbling" onto a website about spiritual topics, or "running into" someone they didn't see very often who invited them to a Bible study "out of the blue."

> Evangelism occurs at the intersection
> of the human and the divine, where
> people do ordinary things . . . and
> God does what only he can do.

Perhaps the most entertaining moment of my interviews came when Alice told me how seeing a squirrel jump prompted her to become a Christian. She had attended several weeks' worth of Christian meetings on campus (which she heard about just "randomly" walking across campus and seeing a table with information on it about the group) and processed what she thought about the gospel. One of the staff workers of the group had shared the gospel with her, but she didn't respond at that time. Now, sitting alone, at a secluded spot on campus, she wondered what was holding her back from crossing from unbelief to belief.

She told me her whole story with hardly any emotion in her voice or change in her facial expressions. Then all of a sudden, as if prompted by a loud noise, she sat up straight in her chair, laughed a bit, and said, "I was sitting down and I saw a bunch of squirrels. They were making these huge jumps in the air." She moved her hands for the first time in our conversation, showing a huge arc of the squirrels' flights. She laughed again and said, "I thought that was cool, and I was like, 'If a squirrel can make huge jumps like that, there's really nothing standing in my way. I can do this. I can accept Jesus.'"

A Supernatural Process

We need to reflect on the supernatural dimension of conversion. Evangelism occurs at the intersection of the human and the divine, where people do ordinary things (declare, ask questions, offer evidences, give defenses, share experiences, and so on) and God does what only he can do (open blind eyes, soften hardened hearts, raise the "dead," and the like). We work hard to do our part, and we pray earnestly for God to do his part.

And we need to remember that God's part is supernatural. In the previous chapter I mentioned the seed Jesus spoke of in Mark 4. Let's take a closer look at that parable. Jesus had just talked about seeds that landed on different kinds of soils. But then he told another parable about just a single seed. The former parable shines the light on the diversity of experiences people have after hearing the gospel. But this second parable emphasizes the relentless work of God upon the seed that falls on good soil.

> This is what the kingdom of God is like. A man scatters seed on the ground. Night and day, whether he sleeps or gets up, the seed sprouts and grows, though he does not know how. All by itself the soil produces grain—first the stalk, then the head, then the full kernel in the head. As soon as the grain is ripe, he puts the sickle to it, because the harvest has come. (Mark 4:26–29)

I imagine this could prompt laziness on our part. "God's going to save whoever he wants to, with or without our help," we might declare with a not-so-slight tone of piety. But Jesus also commanded us to go "preach the gospel to all creation" (Mark 16:15), so let's not give ourselves such a lame excuse. Instead, let's allow this teaching to embolden us. If in fact God produces growth—night and day, whether we sleep or get up—let's proclaim boldly and watch God work.

As J. I. Packer keenly observes, "The sovereignty of God in grace gives us our only hope of success in evangelism. . . . Were it not for the sovereign grace of God, evangelism would be the most futile and useless enterprise that the world has ever seen."[1]

That's why Jesus taught that the new birth is like the wind. "The wind blows wherever it pleases. You hear its sound, but you cannot tell where it comes from or where it is going. So it is with everyone born of the Spirit" (John 3:8). Now I imagine that some people trained in meteorology might say that we *do* know about wind direction. But that would miss Jesus's point and ignore his use of metaphor. When we stand in the path of wind, there is no doubt that wind is blowing, but there is a sense of mystery about where it's coming from and where it's blowing to. Even if we could determine the direction, we also sense that, at any second, the wind could change direction or slow down or gust up. Wind displays a mix of the known and the unknown. And Jesus's analogy about conversion parallels that mix.

Perhaps another story might illustrate the point. My interview with Betsy might have warranted the title, "Every parent's worst nightmare." Within the first ten minutes of our conversation, I heard about lots of drugs ("weed, LSD, ya know, stuff like that"), lots of alcohol, lots of sex, and three weekends in a row that all involved police. And all this occurred before she turned seventeen! The first of the three weekends resulted in a speeding ticket. On the second weekend, she was arrested for shoplifting and went to jail. The third weekend's reckless driving and numerous other illegal activities brought her before a judge. Amazingly, "He let me go. He thought I looked like 'a pretty good kid.'" But all this made Betsy wonder if she might lose her scholarship to Harvard, where she was to begin her freshman year just four months after that fateful trio of weekends.

When I asked people an open-ended question like, "Tell me how you became a Christian," it was instructive for me to see how they began. Betsy started with, "All right. My family was, like, Christian-ish, but we stopped going to church when I was in fourth grade. And then in middle school, I decided it [Christianity] was stupid and I didn't believe in it. And one of the reasons is because my parents got divorced [when I was] in sixth grade."

For the next fifteen minutes she wove together two recurring themes: intellectual study about whether Christianity was true and sexual promiscuity to an alarming level. She kept going back and forth between the two without making any logical connections. One minute it was, "For some reason I just started thinking about religion again, and I kind of just got more mad at Christianity for being a lie that people believed." The next minute it was, "It wasn't one guy in the picture. It was tons of guys in the picture and absolutely partying a ton."

After the third weekend of arrests, she felt like "God was trying to get my attention. I was reading books like *The Case for Christ* and was reading his [author Lee Strobel's] entire bibliography and read all the things he referenced. The more I researched it, the more I was convinced that I was wrong." However, during that same time, "I just kind of said to myself, 'OK, I'm gonna try to be a better person now. I'm gonna try to stop drinking and not hook up with as many people and, ya know, try to be nicer." But she couldn't do it.

Then, one day, while smoking a cigarette in her backyard ("My mom wouldn't let me smoke in the house"), her next-door neighbor came out and invited her to a Bible study. At this point, our conversation went something like this.

Me: Wait. How did she invite you to a Bible study?

Betsy: She said, "Would you like to come to a Bible study?" [She added a facial expression that seemed to say, "Well, duh!"]

Me: But those weren't the first words she said, right? Didn't she start with, "Hi. How are you? Isn't this a nice day? How's your cigarette?"

Betsy: No, "Would you like to come to a Bible study?" were her first words. It was totally random.

Me: OK. But you already knew her, right? You had some kind of relationship?

Betsy: Not really. I mean, I saw her before but we hardly ever talked. Maybe I had said hello three times in the last six years.

Me: OK. Was she around your same age, seventeen?

Betsy: Oh, no. She was way older. She was twenty-six—totally un-
         relatable. [And all of the other women in the Bible study
         were much older!]

Me: So, what did you say when this old lady invited you to a
         Bible study?

Betsy: I said, "I would love to come to a Bible study."

Me: Wait. Did you really say you'd "love" to? Did you use that
         word, "love"?

Betsy: Yeah.

Me: Why?

Betsy: Because I had been reading the Bible for like a year and a
         half at that point. And all the guys I was hooking up with
         were a bunch of jerks. So I figured a Bible study might help.

A Bible study did indeed help. She became a Christian that summer and went off to college intent to leave her old self behind. She
found a campus Christian fellowship and began attending meetings
and Bible studies right away.

> On the surface, people may look
> uninterested, hardened, self-satisfied, or
> irredeemable. But God works far below.

Do you see why I think Betsy's story illustrates the supernatural dynamic of conversion and the hidden wind-like work of God
to draw people to himself? From all outward appearances, Betsy
seemed happy with her party lifestyle. Her neighbor could have felt
intimidated to invite such a young "lost soul" to her old-lady Bible
study. On the surface, people may look uninterested, hardened, self-
satisfied, or irredeemable. But God works far below. Through the
convicting, enlightening, and softening work of the Holy Spirit,
together with the two-edged sword of God's Word, the impossible
becomes reality.

Against All Odds

If we forget about God's supernatural power to save, we can find plenty of data to discourage us.

Charles Taylor has convinced us we live in a secular age. In fact, we're not just secular—we're "secular 3." Secular 1 occurred when we emptied our public life of God. Secular 2 followed when fewer and fewer people pursued religion privately. Now, Taylor argues, we're in secular 3, where we've moved from "a society where belief in God is unchallenged and indeed, unproblematic, to one in which it is understood to be one option among others, and frequently not the easiest to embrace."[2] Haven't we gone even further than Taylor's secular 3? Might we find ourselves in secular 4, where religion is not just one option among others but a bad option? Increasingly, people blame religion for the problems of our world. We Christians are intolerant, narrow-minded, homophobic bigots, goes the rant, and our world would be better without our fanaticism.

Social scientists Robert Putnam and David Campbell summed up their research to help us see our time as a period following "a shock and two aftershocks."[3] The shock was the cultural (especially sexual) upheaval of the 1960s. The first aftershock was "the rise of evangelicals and then of the Religious Right." The second aftershock came when people rejected the Religious Right. "In effect," Putnam and Campbell concluded, "many of these Americans, who might have been religiously inclined, but were liberal on moral issues, said 'if that's what religion is all about, then it's not for me.'"[4] They claim that "polarization and pluralism are the principal themes in the recent history of American religion."[5]

Researchers like The Pew Research Center tell us that the United States is becoming less religious, with one of the most significant trends being the dramatic rise of "nones," people who claim no religious affiliation at all. In just seven years, from 2007 to 2014, the number of nones rose from 16 percent to 23 percent of the American population, almost four times the number of adherents to all non-Christian faiths—Jewish, Muslim, Buddhist, Hindu, and other world religions—combined.[6]

Even someone as upbeat as Tim Keller admits, "It's difficult to publicly identify as a Christian believer in a secular age that pressures people to keep their religious beliefs private."[7]

Am I suggesting we ignore these trends or refuse to observe them carefully? Far from it. We must discern the times and adapt our gospel presentations accordingly. We must remember that each of these so-called difficulties presents tremendous opportunities.

I believe Charles Taylor's analysis of our secular age rings true. But I also believe the emptiness of a secular life makes people hunger for the transcendent. We may even find ourselves in something like "secular 5" sometime soon. But it may only leave people more dissatisfied with a nonspiritual existence. Several pastors I know tell me that total strangers regularly "just show up" to their Sunday morning worship services, having found their church through Yelp. Let's not allow the secularity of our age to discourage us. We have living water to satisfy the thirst of secular people, who have "forsaken [God], the spring of living water, and have dug their own cisterns, broken cisterns that cannot hold water" (Jer. 2:13).

> The arrows on charts of religious interest
> may point downward at this moment
> in time, but God has ways to cause
> chart makers to revamp their work.

Putnam and Campbell's schematic of "a shock and two aftershocks" gives us insight to attitudes behind questions. Their research helps us understand the emotional resistance that can seem to thwart reasonable arguments. But we must not allow cultural upheavals to discourage us into thinking we face insurmountable odds. Instead, they can help us grow in empathy as we reach out with a gospel that reaches whole people with boundless grace.

I dig into Pew Research reports and other studies diligently, and I hope you will too. We must know what people around us believe.

Current trends inform in tremendously helpful ways. But, like mutual fund reports, "past performance is no guarantee of future results." The arrows on charts of religious interest may point downward at this moment in time, but God has ways to cause chart makers to revamp their work. He has done so many times in the past. When Josiah was still a youth, he was used by the Lord to bring about a revival that reversed long-standing evil practices that kept people far from God (see 2 Chron. 34:3 and the rest of the chapter). When Ezra brought out the book of the law, rediscovered after a long period of neglect, people stood to hear it read, as if it was the best news they'd ever heard (see Neh. 8).[8] We dare not allow current trends to discourage us from proclaiming words that can defy and reverse those trends.

Here's a story about a student who was not part of my research project. A good friend once asked him about his religious beliefs. He chose to answer in an elaborate letter which included:

> You ask me my religious views: you know, I think, that I believe in no religion. There is absolutely no proof for any of them, and from a philosophical standpoint Christianity is not even the best. All religions, that is, all mythologies to give them their proper name are merely man's own invention—Christ as much as Loki. Primitive man found himself surrounded by all sorts of terrible things he didn't understand—thunder, pestilence, snakes et cetera: what more natural than to suppose that these were animated by evil spirits trying to torture him. These he kept off by cringing to them, singing songs and making sacrifices et cetera. Gradually from being mere nature-spirits these supposed being[s] were elevated into more elaborate ideas, such as the old gods: and when man became more refined he pretended that these spirits were good as well as powerful.
>
> Thus religion, that is to say mythology grew up. . . . Of course, mind you, I am not laying down as a certainty that there is nothing outside the material world: considering the

discoveries that are always being made, this would be foolish. Anything may exist: but until we know that it does, we
can't make any assumptions. The universe is an absolute
mystery: man has made many guesses at it, but the answer
is yet to seek. Whenever any new light can be got as to such
matters, I will be glad to welcome it. In the meantime I am
not going to go back to the bondage of believing in any old
(and already decaying) superstition.[9]

I'm delighted to tell you that student was C. S. Lewis, when he was
seventeen years old. Yes, the same C. S. Lewis who later wrote The
Chronicles of Narnia, *Mere Christianity*, and all those other great
works to help people consider that perhaps Christianity is something
other than a mere "superstition."

By now you may wonder whether or not this book has been mis-
titled. Is any conversion really "unlikely"? Is anyone beyond God's
ability to convert? We can sometimes be fooled (and discouraged)
into thinking that people are too far gone. But that would be to lose
sight of the Scripture's reminder: "There is no wisdom, no insight, no
plan that can succeed against the LORD" (Prov. 21:30). And let's be
quick to ask ourselves, "Is anything too hard for the LORD?" (Gen.
18:14).

When I came to the end of my interview with Erika, the young
woman who took her Bible to Paris, I asked her my standard final
question about the three most important factors in her story. "Definitely my grandfather," she blurted out immediately. She hadn't mentioned him for almost an hour.

"Had he ever talked to you about God?" I asked her.

"No. My father wouldn't have allowed that." She paused and then
added, "But I always admired him and knew he was a man of faith."
In ways she couldn't explain, he played the most significant part in
the supernatural work God chose to do in her life.

I almost wanted to stand and cheer. In my head, I *did* cheer: "Way
to go, Grandpa! Your hours on your knees were worth it."

BRAINSTORMS: PRAYING WITH PEOPLE

While it may seem like the last thing you should do, in some cases, praying with nonbelievers can be powerful. People who are inquiring need to know of the supernatural nature of their search. Offering to pray with people could propel them toward belief better than answers, discussions, or proclamations. Here are a few ways to venture into these intercessions:

- We've been talking for quite a while. I hope this has been helpful. But there's more to faith than just having answers. I wonder if you'd be OK with my praying for you right now—for God to make himself known to you.
- Sometimes people ask God to answer the questions that people can't. Could we just pause right now to ask God to do that for you? I'll pray and you can just join me silently. Or you could pray out loud if you want.
- Are you at the point where you can pray something like this: "God, if you're really there, can you help me know you?"
- I've been praying for you for a long time. At this point, how would you want me to pray?

SEGUE:
THE POWER OF STORY

Stories permeate the Bible. They shape the Scriptures. If we compare the Bible to a quilt, stories are the individual panels, woven together to display a grander picture. The Bible tells one grand narrative by intertwining hundreds of subnarratives. We read the Bible's story and find ourselves caught up in it. Our individual stories reflect, retell, and resonate with God's story.

All that sounds a bit theoretical, doesn't it? I should have told a story to illustrate my point.

Here's one: Maureen grew up in a home that expressed the Christian faith as a set of rules. She didn't do well at keeping them. In fact, one time when only eight years old, she broke a rule in her Christian school and had to sit in the principal's office for several hours as penance. Then the principal told her God loves her anyway. She came home confused. Her parents responded by transferring her to a public school. She told me she went from being "a bad kid in a Christian school to a good kid in a public school."

There she fell in love with drama and acted in several school productions. In high school, she joined the Thespians' Club and starred in numerous musicals and a few serious dramas. In college, she majored in film production and loved the ways stories captivated her heart.

Some friends invited her to a Christian retreat, and because she liked them, she thought a weekend away with them would be fun. On that retreat, she heard a Bible story that changed her life.

Now, if I asked you which Bible story you thought that might be, I think I could guess some of your possible nominees:

- The return of the prodigal son
- The feeding of the five thousand

93

- David's victory over Goliath
- Moses parting the Red Sea

Would you believe me if I told you the story came from Ezekiel 16? Would you know what story that is? Can you even remember the last time you read Ezekiel? Chapter 16 is a horrible story! I find it hard to read without some level of disgust, tears, and anger. And I am certain I've never heard anyone suggest it for its evangelistic appeal at a weekend retreat.

Here's a brief summary of the story. (But I urge you to read the entire chapter—all sixty-three verses.)

"The word of the LORD came" to Ezekiel to tell of God's condemnation of Jerusalem for her adulterous pursuit of other gods. God speaks in the first person of how "I" found "you" (Jerusalem) abandoned as a newborn in a field, covered in her own blood, "your cord . . . not cut" (v. 4), helpless, left to die. But God rescued her. And he didn't stop there: "I made you grow like a plant of the field. You grew and developed and entered puberty" (v. 7).

Ezekiel uses lavish language to depict a beautiful love story. God poured out his love on his bride. "I clothed you with an embroidered dress and put sandals of fine leather on you. I dressed you in fine linen and covered you with costly garments. I adorned you with jewelry: I put bracelets on your arms and a necklace around your neck, and I put a ring on your nose, earrings on your ears and a beautiful crown on your head. So you were adorned with gold and silver; your clothes were of fine linen and costly fabric and embroidered cloth" (vv. 10–13a).

And on and on it goes with the most luxurious of descriptions of God's love. He even marries Jerusalem by "spread[ing] the corner of my garment over you. . . . I gave you my solemn oath and entered into a covenant with you . . . and you became mine" (v. 8).

But then the story turns ugly beyond belief. "You trusted in your beauty and used your fame to become a prostitute. You lavished your favors on anyone who passed by and your beauty became his" (v. 15).

And on and on *this* goes, using words you wouldn't want read in your church's worship service without an extensive warning letter sent to parents, urging them to leave their children home that week.

The word *prostitute* occurs eleven times in this chapter, more than any single chapter in the rest of the Bible. And it gets worse: "And you took your sons and daughters whom you bore to me and sacrificed them as food to the idols" (v. 20). And this is only the first twenty verses of this painful saga. We're not even halfway through the story.

This was the story that Maureen said changed her life! She told me, "It was like hearing how we prostitute ourselves to everything . . . when our real husband is Jesus. We prostitute ourselves to every-thing else. We love everything else except Jesus." It was during this retelling of the story that she "came to the conclusion that I was a sinner. I realized the gravity of my sin."

Ezekiel 16 ends with these astonishing words: "Yet I will remem-ber the covenant I made with you in the days of your youth, and I will establish an everlasting covenant with you . . . and you will know that I am the LORD." Then God adds that he will "make atonement for you for all you have done" (vv. 60, 62–63).

I wasn't surprised that Maureen was an actress. She told her story with dramatic flair and a lot of emotion. She choked back tears at several points, remembering that weekend retreat. But it wasn't during that Ezekiel 16 message or even during that weekend that she became a Christian. At that point, she only saw the extent of her sin, something far worse than breaking her Christian elementary school's rules; and her need for forgiveness, which sitting for a few hours in the principal's office could never accomplish.

Another story brought her to the point of surrender. "Two weeks later I went home for Thanksgiving and just randomly" watched the movie version of C. S. Lewis's *Voyage of the Dawn Treader*. Some-how the dramatic image of the Christ figure, Aslan, standing in front of ocean waves and exercising power over nature—"the way God exercises authority over his kingdom," she told me—made her see her need to repent of her sin and trust in Christ's saving work.

At this point in our conversation, I was frankly skeptical. Was this genuine saving faith or an emotional response to two overly dramatic stories? However, without recounting the rest of my interview (interrogation?), I became convinced that Maureen truly did become a Christian. It was through the unique power of story that God drew her to himself. For Maureen, drama cracked through where rules could not. And I'm convinced she's not alone.

The Nature of Story

I began this chapter with the observation that the Bible consists of stories. Have you ever wondered why that is? What do stories do that propositions do not?

Stories engage. They stimulate imagination. They melt resistance. They charm and delight and enable us to grasp concepts at deeper levels than we could through lectures.

Please hear me carefully: I'm not rejecting propositions. I could not have made that point without stating one. I cringe when I hear people say we should only tell stories and quit making arguments. Sadly, I've never been able to make an argument that convinced those people they were violating their own dogmatic proposition. Yes, Jesus told stories: "There was a man who had two sons . . ." (Luke 15:11). But he also made declarations: "Blessed are the poor in spirit, for theirs is the kingdom of heaven" (Matt. 5:3).

The Bible is made up of a variety of genres—
poetry, propositions, prophecy, and,
perhaps more than all the others, stories.

Our current cultural mood seems to love stories and disdain propositions. The Bible makes no such dichotomy. We must see that the Bible is made up of a variety of genres—poetry, propositions, prophecy, and, perhaps more than all the others, stories. The diverse genres work in a variety of ways.

Earlier I argued that we are multifaceted people who respond to a multifaceted gospel. For the same reason, we respond to a variety of literary genres. We are more than idea-processors. Thus we need (not just enjoy) stories, poems, prophecies, and other modes of expression.

The Telling of Stories

Hearing stories changes us. So does telling them. When I set up my interviews with recent converts, I made sure to ask them for no less than forty-five minutes of their time. It takes that long to get beyond just the facts.

I started noticing a trend: after thirty-five minutes, people began to notice things they hadn't seen before. It almost became comical how often I heard them say things like:

"Oh—I don't think I ever noticed this, but . . ."

"Wow, I just realized . . ."

"Hey, I just remembered something I left out . . ."

My interviews consistently fell into three parts. People first told me their story the way they wanted to. That took ten to fifteen minutes. I then asked for clarification about a few things and asked some questions my interviewees hadn't answered yet. That took another twenty to thirty minutes. During the third section, I had them go back and "just tell me more about" things they'd already discussed. It was during this final section that they started seeing connections between parts of their story or remembering things they had left out. And it was during these times that they shifted from recounting to appreciating, and from description to doxology.

Several people used the word *afresh* toward the end of our time together. One man said it like this: "I'm really glad I got to talk about this. It helps me see afresh all that God has done for me."

By way of application, I encourage church leaders to interview new members for longer than a few minutes, through face-to-face conversations. Electronic questionnaires have their place, and I don't want to discourage that approach to research; we need both quantitative and qualitative modes. But for helping people grow in grace and appreciating the riches of God's work in their lives (see

Eph. 1:18), having them tell their stories at length can help in unexpected ways.

> We need to tell a wide range of narratives—
> not just the sensational ones. In fact, what
> we consider a less dramatic story might
> actually connect with more people.

Encouraging people to tell their conversion stories can expand our evangelistic reach as well. When non-Christians hear stories of people coming to faith, they sometimes imagine themselves in the stories they hear. They might think, "Yeah . . . I can see myself doing that someday," or "Me too! I thought I was the only one who thought that, or had that question, or faced that problem." Some may think, "If that person could become a Christian, I can too." Different people relate to and respond to different kinds of stories. We need to tell a wide range of narratives—not just the sensational ones. In fact, what we consider a less dramatic story might actually connect with more people.

Of course, we should work with people to help them tell their stories well. Conversion testimonies used to be standard fare at evangelistic crusades or campus outreach meetings. A speaker would preach or present an apologetic message to convince the minds of outsiders. Then an "ordinary" Christian would share his or her testimony—usually for no more than three to five minutes. That dual approach connected on numerous levels. I'd like to see a return to that recipe for outreach.

Hearing conversion narratives also encourages believers to reach out with boldness. Many Christians are reluctant to evangelize, falling into the trap of seeing their acquaintances as too far gone for God to save. When we hear testimonies, we reenergize our evangelistic zeal, sensing that "if God could save that person . . . well, is anyone too far gone?"

Weaving Our Story with the Gospel Story

We could share our testimony through the tried-and-true pattern of

- what our life was like before coming to faith;
- the circumstances through which we came to faith; and
- how our life is different now that we have come to faith.[1]

But I think we can do better than that. When Paul shared his testimony before King Agrippa in Acts 26, he gave us a more complex model to follow. It blends together his experiences, some pre-evangelistic prompters, a few doctrinal elements, a dash of apologetics, and even a call for a decision. While Agrippa did not respond as Paul had hoped (and prayed!—see his comment in v. 29), and accused Paul of losing his mind (v. 24), I think we should still follow Paul's example.

Note that the text calls Paul's speech a "defense" (v. 1). That's probably a better description than a "testimony," since offering a defense is probably a better goal for us than merely sharing our story.

Consider these ingredients in Paul's speech:

- *Pre-evangelistic plausibility.* Toward the beginning, he asked, "Why should any of you consider it incredible that God raises the dead?" (v. 8). He wanted them to see that his line of argument fit with beliefs they already held. This is a crucial step for many people. Sometimes they need to own up to their own faith positions and see that ours are not that different. Some people need to consider that something *might* be true before they accept that it *is* true.
- *Selective details about his personal experience.* Paul told about his upbringing (vv. 4–5), his recent opposition to the gospel (vv. 9–11), his Damascus road drama (vv. 12–18), and some (but not many!) details of what happened after his conversion (vv. 20–21). Any recounting of an event is selective. You can't include everything—if for no other reason than people don't want to hear it all. In some instances you may have five minutes

to tell your story. That's probably the max. In most cases, it's more like one or two minutes. So it's worth thinking through several different-length messages: the one-minute "elevator" version, the two-minute "walking down the hallway together" version, the three-minute "over a cup of coffee" version, and so on. If people ask for more, then it's time to elaborate—with one eye on the clock and the other on their face. If they show signs of losing interest, it's time to move toward dialogue and away from monologue. Paul's situation allowed for a longer presentation. Our short statements could open doors for fuller explanations.

- *Doctrinal statements of gospel components.* Paul wove into his narrative the facts that his message calls people "from darkness to light, and from the power of Satan to God" (v. 18), provides forgiveness of sins (v. 18), leads to "a place among those who are sanctified" (v. 18), requires faith in Jesus (v. 18), includes the need for repentance (v. 20), and must be validated by deeds (v. 20). It is not manipulative for us to follow Paul's example and intertwine our experiences with what we learned along the way. Statements that begin with "here's what happened," and "here's what I learned," and "here's what I understood" can all be included in our defense.

- *Apologetic arguments.* Paul attempted to persuade (not merely inform) Agrippa and "all who [were] listening" (v. 29) that his message was "nothing beyond what the prophets and Moses said would happen" (v. 22). His message implied, "You should believe this because it's reasonable," not "You should appreciate this and celebrate diversity because it's my experience and knowing a lot of different perspectives will make you a well-rounded person." If we only tell of subjective experiences, we are unwittingly adopting our culture's relativistic worldview. If we also express objective truth, we tacitly call for a decision.

If you're thinking this might take some preparation, you're right. Very few of us could be this brilliant on the spot. We don't have any indication from the text that Paul came up with this spontaneously.

While it might be best to *sound* unrehearsed, some diligent fore-thought and practice doesn't sound unreasonable.

> We need to tell people what caused
> us to believe, but we also need to say,
> "Here's why I'm glad that I did."

Here are a few more suggestions as you prepare your story (or, better still, your defense):

- *Use paper and pen.* There's nothing like writing things down to move you toward clarity. Even though you'll eventually deliver this message orally, the starting point should be in writing.
- *Remember and edit.* Make a list of all the events and details that contributed toward the path God used in your life. Then start crossing things off the list. Decide which events were really pivotal and which were merely incidental. Prioritize those details that clarify the gospel message.
- *Recall lessons and corrections.* Which facts, evidences, and arguments corrected your wrong thinking about God, Jesus, eternal life, and so forth? Weave those into your story with phrases like, "I never understood that ____," or "I found out that ____," or "I realized I had been wrong about ____."
- *Combine truth and goodness.* The gospel is true, but it's also good. People need to hear about both. A good defense helps hearers understand and appreciate, become informed and hungry, and say, "Now I understand," as well as, "How can I experience that?" We need to tell people what caused us to believe, but we also need to say, "Here's why I'm glad that I did."

These short defenses could pave the way for longer discussions. As those dialogues convey our salvation message, we want people to know it includes repentance, forgiveness, fulfillment of prophecy, and eternal life as well as joy, relief, comfort, power to live a good life, hope, and a host of other benefits. They tell a better story than the ones people have heard or built their lives around.

By God's grace, some people may respond better than Agrippa did to Paul.

The first half of this book has focused on hearing people's stories of coming to faith and what we can learn from them. The second half will now shift the spotlight more on how we should proclaim the best story people can ever hear.

PART 2

How Christians Can Proclaim Good News

CHAPTER 5

Carefully

Not long ago, a friend of mine and I decided to check out a new golf course, having heard great things about its scenic layout. Upon entering the clubhouse, we asked how much the greens fees were. The golf pro told us the price and added, "And that includes your cart." My friend countered, "Oh, we're going to walk. How much does it cost without a cart?" I'll never forget the facial expression on that formerly friendly man. It blended incredulity, horror, and pain. "Have you ever played this course?" he asked us. "No, sir," we both offered in unison. "Ohhh. This course is awfully long. I'd warn you not to walk it."

Naively, we shrugged off his warning. "That's OK," we assured him. "We need the exercise."

After grabbing our clubs, we walked to the first tee, where the club's starter approached us to check our paid receipts. (This is standard precedure at most courses. They want to make sure you don't just walk on without paying.) But rather than ask to see those pieces of paper, he said, "Hey, you forgot your cart. You need to go over there and get your cart." We told him that we were walking the course.

It's remarkable to see the same complex facial expression on two different faces within just minutes of each other. But there it was— that trifecta of incredulity, horror, and pain. "Ohhh. This course is awfully hilly. I'd warn you not to walk it."

Again, we shrugged off the warning. But this time we noticed a drop in our enthusiasm for our upcoming workout. As we walked past the guard (who by now was shaking his head and laughing at us), my friend said to me, "I wonder if this is a mistake. One guy warned us the course is long. The other guy told us it's hilly."

It was a huge mistake! By the fourth hole, we were arguing about who was supposed to bring the oxygen tanks.

When you get a warning, danger probably lurks nearby. If you get several warnings about the same danger, you probably should heed them.

> "Do not be deceived" may be one of the most frequent commands in all of Scripture.

We get a lot of warnings in the Bible about getting the gospel wrong. It must be a real danger. "Do not be deceived" may be one of the most frequent commands in all of Scripture. The many warnings start by telling us to look out for false prophets. They continue by outlining the nature of deception. And they culminate with specific cautions about missing the unique message of the gospel.

I'll offer just a few samples of each of these warnings, but I urge you to dig in for yourself and see the recurring theme and feel the dire urgency throughout the Bible.

Jeremiah warned, "Do not listen to what the prophets are prophesying to you; they fill you with false hopes. They speak visions from their own minds, not the mouth of the LORD" (Jer. 23:16).

Jesus echoed Jeremiah's words and ramped up the imagery: "Watch out for false prophets. They come to you in sheep's clothing, but inwardly they are ferocious wolves" (Matt. 7:15). These false prophets will increase in number as time goes on (24:11), performing great signs and miracles for the very purpose of deceiving (v. 24).

Peter warns us against both false prophets and false teachers (2 Peter 2:1). Paul warns against being "blown here and there by every wind of teaching and by the cunning and craftiness of people in their deceitful scheming" (Eph. 4:14).

This danger is not just from without. We can even deceive ourselves (see 1 Cor. 3:18 and James 1:26). This shouldn't surprise us. We must remember that our problem began through deception in the garden, as the woman said: "The serpent deceived me, and I ate" (Gen. 3:13). The deception certainly didn't stop there. It continues to mess us up, leading to a hardening that gets worse and worse (see Heb. 3:13).

Leaders in particular are commissioned with the task of shepherding God's people by protecting them against those who "distort the truth" (Acts 20:30). They are to "encourage others by sound doctrine and refute those who oppose it" (Titus 1:9).

And then we come to the book of Galatians, an entire treatise against a very specific kind of deception—the danger of believing "a different gospel" (Gal. 1:6). It's easy to read Galatians and think, "How could those people be so stupid? I see why Paul calls them 'foolish'" (3:1). We might even be tempted to wonder why people who are so easily thrown into confusion (see 1:7) get a whole book of the Bible showcasing their odd mistake.

But just a short time living the Christian life, and an even shorter period of honest reflection, should lead us to realize that we all share the Galatian tendency toward replacing the true gospel with another one, "which is really no gospel at all" (1:7).

Paul ramps up the warning against mere garden-variety deception to the unique problem of being "bewitched" (3:1), using a word found nowhere else in the New Testament. Falling for another gospel goes beyond mere intellectual confusion. As New Testament scholar Douglas Moo points out, "While it is unlikely that Paul means to say that the Galatians are under a spell cast by a sorcerer, his choice of this word does suggest that the Galatians' turnaround in their thinking can only be explained by recourse to an evil spiritual influence."[1]

It must be easy to be deceived and fall for another gospel. No wonder we get so many warnings against it. I'll say more about the most common non-gospels later in this chapter.

False Testimonies

Not all of my interviews led me to sing songs of praise. I heard several "conversion narratives" that had a different conversion than one centered on the cross. In addition to the minor disappointment that these conversations would not qualify for my research project, I felt profound sadness that these people had heard and embraced a false gospel.

A few of them told me how they finally came to the point when they realized their lives needed to change. They drank too much or slept around too much or did drugs too much and ended up "really, really unhappy." On campuses where partying and promiscuity are the norm, these tired souls found odd alternatives in Christian fellowships. For this we can offer much gratitude.

But their stories turned on personal decisions to stop drinking, stop having sex, break up with a girlfriend or boyfriend, or "live my life the way God wants me to live," not on repentance, regeneration, and trust in the finished work of the cross. Some told me their lives changed when their schedules changed. They stopped going to parties and instead "never missed" a prayer meeting. They gave up sex and alcohol and took up singing and prayer. As they talked, I found myself profoundly thankful for the destruction they averted but also disappointingly perplexed. I kept waiting to hear something about Jesus.

Even after prompting them with questions about why Jesus had to die or what part he played in their lifestyle changes, their answers stayed in the category of vague. In four specific cases, I turned off my recorder, put away my notebook, took out a piece of paper, and drew a diagram that had a big cross in the middle. Sadly, it seemed to me that this was an unfamiliar concept for some of them.

> We must choose our words thoughtfully,
> understanding the Scriptures, and
> circumspectly, understanding the times.

Two interviewees described a different experience than the "I cleaned up my act" variety. For them, "becoming a Christian" centered on a deeply moving emotional experience. They went on a retreat, spent hours in the woods, listened to hear God's voice, and came back with a sense that God "really, really, really loves me." These two students, in independent interviews, used almost identical vocabulary to tell how "for the first time" they felt loved and had "no doubt" it was God who loved them. Again, I asked about Jesus's death on the cross and, for both of them, this seemed like an odd topic for me to bring up and spoil the mood.

All this leads me to conclude we must be careful in how we proclaim the good news. If Paul asked for prayer "that I may proclaim [the gospel] clearly, as I should" (Col. 4:4), it must be quite possible to proclaim our message *unclearly*. We must choose our words thoughtfully, understanding the Scriptures, and circumspectly, understanding the times. We need to take into account at least four hindrances to clarity: (1) the confusion into which we speak, (2) a contempt for certainty, (3) the challenge of words, and (4) the counterintuitive nature of the gospel. I offer these in no particular order. Depending on your situation and the people you talk to, one or more of these factors may rise to the surface as more significant than the others.

The Confusion into Which We Speak
(Seeking Clarity amid the Chaos)

Places still exist where people have never heard the gospel. But increasingly, many people have heard it and rejected it. They need to hear it again.

Even more people *think* they've heard our message, *presume* they understand it, and think it's irrelevant (or worse). They need to hear it afresh.

We proclaim a precise message into a cloudy atmosphere. Perhaps it's best to think of numerous atmospheres with seemingly limitless variety. I'll zoom in on just two of our message's themes that require extra clarifying: God's love and God's grace.

God's Love

Many people today presume a right standing with God because God loves them. Since he is loving, they assume, he'll not judge them or condemn them. He certainly won't send them to hell. If you're not scared off by theological terms, you can think of this as *presumed salvific love*. Many have heard that God is a "God of love" and they equate that with salvation, though they may not use that particular word. In clarifying the gospel, we need to distinguish between God's universal love for all his creation and his unique saving love for only those who repent and trust his greatest display of love, Jesus's atoning death on the cross.[2]

God's Grace

Grace is frequently misconstrued as something other than the atoning kind.[3] Again, if you don't mind theological terms, it's viewed as *non-propitious grace*. People like a cross-less grace. To be fair to them, the word *grace* does have several legitimate definitions. We say grace before meals. A dancer can be said to move with grace. Some speakers express themselves with grace. Dictonary.com lists as many as twenty-two different definitions for the word.

One helpful distinction can be seen when the Bible speaks of "the grace of our Lord Jesus" (e.g., Acts 15:11). This is not saying that Jesus was a gracious person when he was here on earth (although he most definitely was), or that he did some nice things that could be described as grace (like feeding five thousand hungry people). "The grace of the Lord Jesus Christ" is used to refer to Jesus's unique sin-pardoning, wrath-satisfying, salvation-purchasing, once-for-all-atoning death on the cross and includes his resurrection that followed. It's gospel grace unlike any and every other kind of grace.

A Contempt for Certainty
(Claiming Knowledge in a "Who's to Say?" Culture)

The apostle John liked knowledge. He recorded that Jesus defined eternal life as "that they know you, the only true God, and Jesus Christ, whom you have sent" (John 17:3). He assured the readers of his first epistle that if they "believe in the name of the Son of God" they would "know that [they] have eternal life" (1 John 5:13). This affirmation came after he made many other "we know" statements.[4]

Other voices in Scripture assure us we can know God, know his ways, know of his love, and know about the next life. The very fact that God inspired a book, something we read that leads to a kind of knowledge, must imply that he wants us to know some things.

But we live in a world that not only denies the possibility of knowledge but disdains such a claim. Some of the people we talk to about Jesus may ask, "How do you know that?" and in many cases, they really mean, "How can we know anything?" They assure us we can't be sure of anything (and they sound rather sure of that). We need to find confident ways to defend our confidence.

Please note, I chose to use the word *confidence* rather than *certainty*. In our scientific age, people tend to assume we must have "absolute certainty"—something we can prove in a laboratory—before we should believe something. I find myself relying on Leslie Newbigin's term *proper confidence* as a better vocabulary choice than "absolute certainty."[5] This is not the place to delve into comparative theories of knowledge,[6] but suffice it to say we need to challenge people's knowledge about knowledge before we tell them we can know the God who gave us the ability to know.

> It is remarkable how often the Bible proclaims truth with unwavering confidence.

On the negative side, we can point out that many scientists aren't certain about the things they "know" or "discover" or "prove." I remember hearing a highly esteemed astronomer speak about his work with NASA and their recent mission to Pluto. After nine and a half years of travel, their robotic spacecraft reached Pluto. What this scientist emphasized in his presentation was "how many surprises they had." Many of the things they thought they knew about Pluto proved to be false, and many unexpected truths were discovered. Honest scientists regularly admit the limits of their knowledge and research findings. Absolute certainty is something nonscientists assume they can have because "science proved it." But good scientists aren't so arrogant.

On the positive side, it is remarkable how often the Bible proclaims truth with unwavering confidence. Jesus didn't speak with caveats. If we back off too far in our claims to know God and what he has revealed, we simply dive into the waters of relativism that have left people adrift and rudderless. When would-be evangelists acquiesce and only speak of "what I've found" or "what this means to me" or "how my life has changed," we make it too easy for people to reject our message with the ubiquitous "true for you but not for me" cliché.

We should indeed share our testimonies. That's why I offered instructions about it in the Segue section above. But we must do so as a pointer to what we know and what God wants us to know, not just leave it at what we as individuals have experienced.

One helpful distinction we can offer is that knowing God is different from knowing facts about things. God is a personal being, and knowing a person is different from knowing a planet, or a math equation, or the shortest route to the office. Even people we think we know well surprise us sometimes. We know God because he has opened a way for us to do so through the gospel. We grow in our knowledge of him over time through the many aspects of Christian living, such as praying to him, reading his Word, and living in community with his people.

The Challenge of Words
(Aiming for Specificity in a "Whatever!" World)

At one of my evangelism training seminars, I met a man named Bernard who told me he was a follower of Jesus and that he was Jewish. Coming from a Jewish background myself, I was excited and wanted to hear his conversion story. But I never heard it because he had never converted. He "followed" Jesus by serving meals at a homeless shelter. He "followed" Jesus by loving people sacrificially. And he "followed" Jesus by "not judging anyone."

I meet a lot of Christians who dislike the word *Christian*. They insist on using the phrase "follower of Jesus" instead. I understand their discomfort. In our current culture, many people think the word Christian means hypocrite or homophobe. And I certainly appreciate "follower of Jesus" as an accurate description of what it means to be a Christian.

But my conversation with Bernard highlighted that any and every term needs clarification. When I told him how I became a Christian and how some of my Jewish relatives rejected me, he looked puzzled. When I asked him about his beliefs about Jesus, he used terms like kind, gentle, loving, noncondemning, and accepting. I spoke of atonement, fulfillment of prophecy, forgiveness, and resurrection. As we compared our two stories, we both realized we had come to very different understandings of what "follower of Jesus" meant.

When I asked how his family responded to his faith decision, he told me they were proud of him for working at a homeless shelter. He then went out of his way to tell me that he didn't think his parents needed to believe in Jesus. "Jews don't need to believe in Jesus to go to heaven. That's ridiculous," he told me with not a minor note of condemnation. The rest of our conversation felt strained, and I grieved that the term "follower of Jesus" was not immune to corruption.

> Many people admit they're "broken," but they mean something far less damning than what the Bible means when it speaks of our rebellion, wickedness, idolatry, and sin.

Communication is more difficult than most people realize. We assume that when we say something, our hearers understand us. But in reality, often they don't. That's why bookstores have entire sections devoted to the challenges of interpersonal communication. Alan Alda wrote one with the delightful title *If I Understood You, Would I Have This Look on My Face?*

As we prepare for gospel conversations, we need to consider whether people will accurately grasp the meanings of our key terms.

We must plan to define, clarify, elaborate, illustrate, and consult a thesaurus along with our Bible. This would be true in any culture at any time. But it's particularly important in a day when words are thrown around with little thought or concern for the right definition. People wonder, "Can't we just use words the way we want and ascribe meanings in ways that seem best to us?"

For example, many Christians like the word *brokenness* as a way of expressing the concept of sin. I'm not entirely negative about that term. But it should not be the only word we use to discuss sin. Otherwise people will assume brokenness means something that happened *to* them, not an action done *by* them. Many people admit they're "broken," but they mean something far less damning than what the Bible means when it speaks of our rebellion, wickedness, idolatry, and sin. If we tell a non-Christian, "The Bible says we're broken," I imagine many, if not most, will think, "Yes, I too had a dysfunctional family and have wounds from my childhood, and I still suffer from low self-esteem and shame as a result." I don't deny the likelihood of their situation, but that kind of brokenness doesn't seem to require a cross. Our problem is worse than just brokenness, and the gospel is better than any cross-less solution.

To make matters even trickier, we live in a world where the word *Christian* has been co-opted by some who preach a radically different gospel from their pulpits. Some clergy with seminary degrees, who use "Reverend" as a title, hold positions of influence that make our task more difficult.

For example, consider this interchange during a radio interview between atheist Christopher Hitchens and Marilyn Sewell, a Unitarian minister:[7]

Sewell: The religion you cite in your book is generally the fundamentalist faith of various kinds. I'm a liberal Christian, and I don't take the stories from the Scripture literally. I don't believe in the doctrine of atonement (that Jesus died for our sins, for example). Do you make any distinction between fundamentalist faith and liberal religion?

Hitchens: I would say that if you don't believe that Jesus of Nazareth was the Christ and Messiah, and that he rose again from the dead and by his sacrifice our sins are forgiven, you're really not in any meaningful sense a Christian.

Sewell: Let me go someplace else. When I was in seminary I was particularly drawn to the work of theologian Paul Tillich. He shocked people by describing the traditional God—as you might as a matter of fact—as "an invincible tyrant." For Tillich, God is "the ground of being." It's his response to, say, Freud's belief that religion is mere wish fulfillment and comes from the humans' fear of death. What do you think of Tillich's concept of God?

Hitchens: I would classify that under the heading of "statements that have no meaning—at all."

Thank you, Christopher, for such clarity. Our challenge today includes countering distortions of the gospel that declare: "A god without wrath brought men without sin into a kingdom without judgment through the ministrations of Christ without a cross."[8]

The Counterintuitive Nature of the Gospel
(Proclaiming a Message That Defies Comparison)

Our biggest challenge, however, does not come from our surrounding culture or the complexities of communication. It stems from our very message, the gospel of grace. This gospel is so totally alien to human nature that people have a difficult time grasping it. Our message is counterintuitive, countercultural, counter-merit, counter-almost-everything. So much of life is built upon reward for effort. We write resumes to impress others with our accomplishments. We receive rewards by outperforming others. We win medals for beating opponents.

But we proclaim a message of benefiting from someone else's merits, of getting the exact opposite of what we deserve, of receiving honor when punishment would be more fitting. The gospel of unmerited favor doesn't seem to fit in a world of reward and meritocracy.

The two most common alternatives to the gospel are performance and presumption. Both rest on people's own merits, not those of anyone else. In the first system, if we accomplish certain tasks or practice certain rituals or achieve certain levels of morality, we earn acceptance from God. In the second, we just have that acceptance already because of our inherent goodness. Both systems fail to grasp the perfect standard of God's righteousness and the depths of our failure to reach it.

> Admitting to being wrong doesn't come naturally or easily. No wonder Jude tells us to "be merciful to those who doubt" (v. 22).

At some point, people who come to saving faith have to say to themselves something like, "I've been wrong all my life." Admitting to being wrong doesn't come naturally or easily. No wonder Jude tells us to "be merciful to those who doubt" (v. 22). For both believers and outsiders, the concept of grace is difficult to grasp. We shouldn't be surprised if it takes several discussions before people begin to understand.

I even think we should weave statements like these into our gospel presentations: "I realize this may seem unusual," or "I know this sounds different than what you might have been thinking," or "I understand why this is hard to grasp," or "Hey, I know. This is weird." I fear that some of our evangelistic appeals imply, "C'mon. You should get this already. This is easy to understand."

We can temper our evangelistic impatience by remembering numerous New Testament prayers for understanding. Paul, in particular, regularly prays for saved people to grow in their knowledge of what they already have. If this was so easy to grasp, why the numerous prayers for us to grow in our understanding?

To the Ephesians, Paul writes: "I pray that the eyes of your heart may be enlightened in order that you may know the hope to which he has called you, the riches of his glorious inheritance in his holy people, and his incomparably great power for us who believe" (Eph. 1:18–19). Later in that same letter, he adds: "I pray that you, being rooted and established in love, may have power, together with all the Lord's holy people, to grasp how wide and long and high and deep is the love of Christ, and to know this love that surpasses knowledge" (Eph. 3:17–19). Note that he prays that we would "know" something that "surpasses knowledge." No wonder he prays for us to "have power" for this level of knowledge. And no wonder he offers up this prayer several times. Given that intensity of prayer for those who have already received the gospel, shouldn't we extend kindness and patience toward those who haven't come to that point yet?

The Tensions of Evangelism

By now, you may wonder if evangelism is impossible. My efforts to impress you about how people come to faith from a wide range of starting points, how Scripture describes the gospel in diverse ways, and how many warnings we get against getting the message wrong may overwhelm more than inspire. In addition, you may feel caught between three influential voices in the body of Christ—the zeal of evangelists, the compassion of pastors, and the precision of theologians. You hear reports from missionaries of evangelistic success, read books by pastors on applying the gospel to your life, and listen to podcasts by theologians on the dangers of heresy. How do you line up with all three approaches?

Would it help if I told you I think evangelism *is* impossible? But I will quickly add that God does the impossible—often! We seek to do the best job we can, to constantly improve in our communication skills, to study the Scriptures so we understand the truth better and better. But we rest on the fact that God is the one who draws people to himself, opens blind eyes, softens hardened hearts, and uses our imperfect efforts for his perfect purposes. We do our part in evangelism, and God does his part. And we rest in the fact that his part far outweighs ours.

Perhaps Andrew's story will be an encouragement to you. Raised

in a "ridiculously strict" (his words) Christian home, Andrew tried
to obey all the rules his parents, church, Christian school, and ultra-
conservative Christian college said were God's will. When I met him
for lunch to hear his story, he used the word *ridiculous* several times
and rolled his eyes as he listed some of the standards by which he
was judged. "They even had rules about how men were supposed to
part their hair," he told me. There was something about a neat, clean
separation of hairs that paralleled the separation of Christians from
the world.

The problem was, while Andrew obeyed the minutia, he disobeyed
one rather large commandment. He was gay. He knew it from the
time he was young, and several attempts to date women convinced
him, "No, they're not for me." So he attended strict, legalistic, ultra-
fundamentalist college classes by day and went to gay bars at night.
After graduation, the gay life won and the Christian life faded. He
found a partner he loved, moved in with him, and felt free of the silly
straitjacket of his past. He and his partner even purchased a house
together and enjoyed eight years of faithful partnership.

Sometime during those eight years, Andrew's sister, also raised
in that legalistic world, started attending a church unlike the ultra-
fundamentalist brand of her past. That church struck her as radically
different. The pastor regularly distinguished the gospel of grace from
the message of performance. He preached from passages in the Old
Testament and made it clear that the point of the text was not "Be
like David" or "Be like Moses." "There's a better David and a better Moses who did far more than just give examples to follow," this
pastor taught week after week. In contrast to sermons she had heard
growing up—along the lines of "God is looking for Abrahams in his
world today, people who will take a stand and obey God"—she now
heard, "God sent his Son to be all that Abraham, David, and Moses
were not. This Greater Abraham, Greater David, Greater Moses has
done far more than those men ever could. We don't need to imitate
those people. We need to be remade into new people." She thought
she was hearing a completely different message. She was right.

So she invited Andrew to visit this church. She had not stopped praying for him, even though he had strayed far from God. And Andrew went. He too sensed the contrast between what he heard there and what he had heard in the past. But he wrestled with being gay and being Christian. Was it possible to be both? It was not difficult for him to find several books that argued in favor of being both gay and Christian. Some of them are best sellers. But they failed to convince him that arguments in favor of "loving, monogamous, same-sex marriages" interpreted the Bible accurately. The more he read their attempts, the less convincing they sounded.

So he emailed the pastor of his sister's church and asked to meet with him. He told me all of this in a rather matter-of-fact way. The pastor was a nice guy who listened to Andrew's story, was not shocked by anything he heard, and patiently answered his questions. No, the Bible cannot support the notion that gay sex is God's will. Yes, the gospel message is different than the many alternative "gospels" out there.

Two things stood out to Andrew from his numerous conversations with that pastor. First, the discussions did not center on homosexuality. They were all about the gospel. The two men discussed passages in the book of Romans and, while not ignoring the verses about homosexuality (1:26–27), they spent far more time on the distinctions between grace and works, the gospel and religion, the free gift and the false counterfeits (especially 3:21–31).

The second thing that impressed Andrew was that everyone, not just gays, must come to faith in Jesus and die—die to their own sources of security, their own idols of pleasure, their own methods of salvation. Everyone, whether gay or straight, needs to surrender their sexual authority (themselves!) and submit to God's sexual authority—which includes a narrow plan our world finds ridiculous.

To be sure, the pastor admitted, Andrew's path to faith would involve greater sacrifices than some other people's. He would need to "divorce" his partner, lose a lot of money invested in their house, and even say goodbye to their pets. Jesus wasn't kidding when he insisted, "Whoever wants to be my disciple must deny themselves and take up their cross daily and follow me" (Luke 9:23).

Andrew did indeed leave his former lives—both the legalistic one and the gay one. He told me he has no regrets.

Confident Carefulness

Even after hearing the Bible's many warnings about getting the message right, the great news about proclaiming the good news is that we *can* state it clearly and concisely. We must proclaim it carefully, but we can do so confidently. We must guard against compromise, but we rest in the power of God's Word. We aim for clarity, but we ask the Holy Spirit to illuminate. We rejoice that God uses imperfect proclaimers. And marvel at his perfect results.

BRAINSTORMS: CLARIFICATION

Communication is harder than we realize. If you've ever attended a listening skills workshop, you know you should ask people to restate something you just said. And you also know that it's amazing how far apart their words are from yours. Communicating concepts that are as alien to most people as holiness, sin, forgiveness, atonement, and eternity poses even greater challenges to communication. Here are some ways to move from cloudiness to clarity:

- I realize these topics might be confusing. I certainly don't have them all figured out. Do you have any questions about what we've been talking about?
- Is this making sense?
- Why don't you try to restate what I've been saying in your own words? Maybe that will help us connect better.
- Let me see if I'm understanding the question you just asked me. Are you saying _____?
- Some people find they need a little time to think about these things. Would that be helpful? It might also help if you read some of the Bible on your own. I recommend you check out John's gospel. Here, I'll show you where it is in the Bible.

CHAPTER 6

Fearfully

Many years ago I heard the great jazz genius Ella Fitzgerald sing on *The Tonight Show*. She dazzled the studio audience and millions of television viewers with her ability to swing, sing, and improvise with such ease and fluidity. When she finished with a soaring, long, high final note, the audience erupted. I'll bet even some television viewers applauded in their living rooms.

Then she walked over and sat next to Johnny Carson, the longtime host of the show that launched a thousand careers. She exhaled a sigh of relief and said, "Oh my, I was so nervous." Carson looked stunned. This was Ella Fitzgerald, not some newcomer hoping to break into the world of jazz. This was Ella, The First Lady of Song, the Queen of Jazz, the jazz legend who had sung before millions of people around the world.

Carson stumbled for words and finally said, "Really?" Ella only nodded her head. She was still catching her breath. "But you've sung for audiences thousands of times and probably sung that very song dozens of times!" he tried. Ella simply said, "I'm always scared when I sing."

Apparently her fear didn't hurt her career. And it didn't seem to harm her performance that night either. It seems, for some at least, that the key is not overcoming fear but singing through it.

When I conduct evangelism training workshops, I often get asked, "How do I get past the fear of witnessing?" I usually disappoint people with my answer, "I don't know." I tell them I witness with fear and, so far, God keeps using me as a timid evangelist. I rest in the realization that my confidence is not in my confidence.

Sometimes, I share this story: Not long ago, I arrived home after a very long flight from Los Angeles to Washington, DC. I was thankful to get home after a long weekend of teaching an evangelism class at Talbot School of Theology. My flight had been delayed several times before the six-hour, nonstop marathon of sitting squashed in a seat near the rear of the plane. It was now close to 2:00 a.m. when I climbed into the Uber driver's car for a ride home.

Horrifically, he was chatty! I do want Uber drivers who are alert and awake—but not *that* friendly. He asked me where I had flown in from. "Los Angeles," I offered, hoping my tone of tiredness would convey the unspoken request "I'd like to just sit here and ride." He didn't interpret it that way. "Oh, what brought you out to L.A.?" I wanted to say, "A plane." But I thought that might sound rude. "I taught a class." Again I thought a curt answer would encourage him to concentrate on his driving. "Where?" he inquired.

This was shaping up to be a witnessing opportunity! As I shared what kind of school it was and the subject matter of my course (teaching people to do what I didn't want to do just then), he told me he was a Muslim, "but not a very good one." I prayed a silent prayer of confession I often pray in these kinds of situations. "Lord, forgive me for caring more about my comfort than your glory. I fear his rejection of me far too much. Help me to proclaim the gospel that offers forgiveness of sins to this man—just as it provides forgiveness for my sins—especially the sins of the idolatry of ease and the fear of people." God answers such prayers, and he did indeed give me wisdom about what to say to that man at that late hour.

When the driver told me, "Our religions are the same—except for some things about Jesus," I said, "In a lot of ways, I agree." He looked surprised. Then I added, "But those things about Jesus are pretty big deals." For the rest of the ride, we talked about the unique elements of the gospel, the reality of the resurrection, and the joy of forgiveness of sins—based on Jesus's good work, not our good works. As I got out of the car, I texted him a link to an evangelistic video.[1] I urged him to watch it and consider the message carefully (but not while he's driving!). I urged him to contact me (we had exchanged phone numbers) if he ever wanted to talk. So far, he hasn't reached out or responded to my texts. I still pray for him regularly.

Can God use fearful evangelists?
Apparently he has.

For quite a while, I thought conquering fear was a mandatory prerequisite to fruitful witnessing. I believed God could only use me if I sounded confident and bold. I needed to remember 1 Corinthians 2:3, in which Paul, recounting his ministry in Corinth, wrote, "I came to you in weakness with great fear and trembling." Now, that's my kind of evangelism! Remember that the Lord spoke to Paul in a vision one night during his preaching ministry in that difficult city, saying, "Do not be afraid; keep on speaking, do not be silent" (Acts 18:9). Can God use fearful evangelists? Apparently he has.

Fearfulness might even be an advantage in witnessing. If somehow we've conquered fear and overcome timidity, we might rely on ourselves—our cleverness, our preparedness, our apologetic brilliance, our verbal dexterity. Far better to cry out to God for help, wisdom, strength, and more concern for conveying truth than making a good impression. Fear might be the best prerequisite for the work of evangelism because it keeps us dependent on the One who does the most important work.

I'm always bolstered by recalling the amazing story of Billy Graham's 1957 Madison Square Garden crusade. Most people know of its unlikely success. Opening on May 15, it was planned to go for only six weeks. But the crowds far exceeded expectations. It was "the largest opening-night crowd of any of Graham's American crusades. . . . The *New York Times* devoted two full pages to the first service, including a verbatim transcript of his sermon."[2] Going long past the original plan with packed out crowds every night, Graham and his team decided to conclude the crusade on July 20 with an outdoor event at Yankee Stadium. In 105-degree heat, over one hundred thousand New Yorkers crammed into "the house that Ruth built" to hear a guy with a Southern accent wave his Bible in the air and proclaim, "You must be born again." So Graham and his team extended the crusade again! All the way until Labor Day, when an even larger crowd packed into Times Square one last time.[3]

What many people do not realize was how fearful Graham was at the start of that great run and many other times that summer. Graham biographer William Martin begins his account of the summer of 1957, in a chapter cleverly entitled "God in the Garden," with Billy's vulnerable words: "We face the city with fear and trembling."

"I'm prepared to go to New York to be crucified by my critics, if necessary," Graham said. "When I leave New York, every engagement we have in the world might be canceled."[4] Martin adds, "In spite of all the efforts to generate success [in preparation beforehand] anxiety kept Billy gnawing at his fingernails."[5] In the middle of the summer, when his team decided to broadcast the events on television, Graham "was scared about the money."[6] The entire crusade was so physically exhausting and emotionally draining that by the end of that long summer Graham had lost thirty pounds.[7]

Just as God used Graham in supernatural ways despite his fear and weakness, so too God can use us in mighty ways—even if our knees are knocking and our voice is quivering.

Facing Fear Honestly

Several of the men and women I interviewed told me how hostile to religion they were before someone invited them to a Christian gathering. For example, Tina spent quite a bit of time telling me how turned off she was to church and Christianity after a semester abroad living with a Christian host family. "They kept trying to make me Christian. They put a Bible under my pillow every night . . . and my experience with the church there was definitely not good." Before that semester, she might have considered herself an atheist or an agnostic, but it wasn't something she thought much about. After her semester away, however, she told me, "I was like, 'Religion is literally so bad.'"

By the time she stepped foot back on her campus, she had lots of ammunition against Christians. "Religion was like the Crusades. Religion was the reason for so many wars and horrible things throughout history. All religions suck!" And she let it be known on her dorm floor that she was strongly antireligion. Still, someone bravely invited her to a Bible study! Tina recounted, with a big smile on her face, that weeks later, when she told one of her atheist roommates she was going to a Bible study, all her friend could say was, "You?"

I kept hearing surprise in Tina's voice, echoing the same surprise I heard from many other interviewees. On one campus, three different people named the same person, Brenda, who had invited them, in three completely independent conversations, to the Christian fellowship on campus. When I followed with questions about Brenda, all three told me she was kind of quiet and not really one of "those bold kind of preachers." I wish I had interviewed Brenda and several others who seemingly ignored the hostility or antagonism and invited people to Bible studies.

> The power in evangelism comes from the truthfulness of God's Word, the omnipotence of the Holy Spirit, the sheer goodness of the gospel, and *not* our fearlessness.

We must anticipate some level of opposition when we evangelize. Why else would Jesus tell us we were like "sheep among wolves" (Matt. 10:16). Commenting on this image, Rico Tice, an experienced evangelist, offers, "The Bible tells us to answer those who attack us. But most books I've read on evangelism don't tell you that. There's always this suggestion that if you do evangelism in a certain way, or if you learn to be charming or funny or interesting as you share the gospel, you can avoid getting hit. I want to be honest: if you tell non-Christians about Jesus, it will be painful."[8] In other words, we have good reason for fear. But we must find ways to move forward anyway.

Antidotes to Fear

Replacing Lies with Truth

By now, I hope you sense that I believe we can witness with fear. God can use us even when our voices shake. That's because the power in evangelism comes from the truthfulness of God's Word, the omnipotence of the Holy Spirit, the sheer goodness of the gospel, and *not* our fearlessness.

Nevertheless, we do need to examine our fears and, when possible, get set free from them. Some fears reveal belief of things that are simply untrue. We should take those thoughts captive (see 2 Cor. 10:5) and replace them with truth.

For example, I think many of us assume most people are not interested in spiritual issues or never think about God. You can absorb a lot of pop culture, listen to a wide swath of podcasts, take in a lot of news, and conclude that God is irrelevant to many people. At a bare minimum, God must be content to stay secluded in the realm of private lives and never intrude on polite conversation.

But if God has indeed "set eternity in the human heart" (Eccl. 3:11), it should not surprise us that many people do think about him and wonder how they can know him. I think many of our neighbors would love to talk about substantive things if someone would just ask them. One of my most secular relatives once remarked, when the topic of religion was broached, "I need to talk about these things. I've spent my whole life focused on everything except religion. It's time to change that."

Take another look at pop culture and you'll see a tremendous longing for the transcendent. Listen to music lyrics and see if you don't hear a cry for meaning or purpose or redemption. Consider the tremendous popularity of superhero movies, filled with saviors who rescue a broken world from evil forces. Look at all the movies that predict some kind of apocalyptic end of our world and the need for deliverance.

A recent study conducted by The Pew Research Center reported that "nine out of ten Americans believe in a higher power, but only a slim majority believe in God as described in the Bible." Again, this should not surprise us and, in fact, should encourage us. We can ask people to describe the higher power they believe in and ask them how they arrived at their understanding.

That same study showed that even the nonreligious people are religious! "In the U.S., belief in a deity is common even among the religiously unaffiliated—a group composed of those who identify themselves, religiously, as atheist, agnostic or 'nothing in particular,' and sometimes referred to, collectively, as religious 'nones.' Indeed, nearly three-quarters of religious 'nones' (72%) believe in a higher power of some kind, even if not in God as described in the Bible."[9]

Replacing Vague Generalities with the Specific Gospel

Another untruth that stokes fear is the belief that most people have embraced some form of "moralistic therapeutic deism," a worldview that contradicts the gospel on numerous fronts. The term *moralistic therapeutic deism*, or MTD for short, came on the scene when Christian Smith, an influential sociologist, studied the religious beliefs of teenagers and published several books explaining his findings.

He lists the five points of MTD's "creed" as:

1. A God exists who created and orders the world and watches over human life on earth.
2. God wants people to be good, nice, and fair to each other, as taught in the Bible and by most world religions.
3. The central goal of life is to be happy and to feel good about oneself.
4. God does not need to be particularly involved in one's life except when God is needed to resolve a problem.
5. Good people go to heaven when they die.[10]

An assumption that people hold fast to MTD can scare us away from evangelizing. After all, we may think such a worldview is so complex that we're ill-equipped to dismantle it. Or we may suspect there are too many deeply held convictions for us to overturn. But we should not allow that fear to stifle our evangelistic or pre-evangelistic efforts for at least two reasons.

First, as I conducted my interviews, I found little evidence of something as unified or coherent as MTD. To be sure, many non-Christians believe in some kind of morality or moralism and think everyone should adhere to it. Aside from a very small number of die-hard relativists, most people think some things are right and some things are wrong and people should live accordingly. This is nothing new and no bigger obstacle for us than what God's people have faced for centuries.

I also found that a high regard for therapeutic solutions to life's problems varies more than Smith's model suggests. And deism is a far more precise religious system than most people can articulate. In other words, I find Smith's labels to have more clarity than what most people actually believe. Smith himself admits, "Note that no teenager would actually use the terminology 'Moralistic Therapeutic Deist' to describe himself or herself. That is our summarizing term."[11] Indeed, in summarizing, I believe Smith has overstated the obstacles we face. MTD's bark is worse than its bite.

Second, and far more important, MTD, adhered to by even its most ardent followers, is terribly vague and unsatisfying. It might actually serve as some of the best pre-evangelism we could ever devise. The gospel is magnificent news for MTDers because it sets them free from the impossible demands of moralism. It provides forgiveness, power, and purpose far better than therapy can. It opens the way for them to know God as Abba-Father, Redeemer-King, Savior, and Lord, which is infinitely better than anything deism has to offer. The gospel saves people; MTD only compounds their lostness.

Replacing Prowess with Humility

Fear can stymie our witness if we think we must have answers for every possible question people might pose. "What if they ask me something I can't answer?" has caused more cases of spiritual lock-jaw than we can imagine. We *should* do our homework and prepare ourselves to "give an answer to everyone who asks" (1 Peter 3:15). But we should also expect that people will ask us some questions we haven't studied yet. We *will* be asked questions we can't answer. Count on it. But that's not a problem. In fact, it might help in more powerful ways than having all the answers. When people ask a question we don't know how to answer, we should offer some of the best apologetic words ever: "I don't know." This shows humility and a high regard for the person we're talking to. It shows respect for them and their questions. When we ask for time to think about their question and do some research, it builds a bridge of compassion better than some tightly crafted answers might.

A Real and Present Danger

One fear must receive our utmost respect—the fear of compromising the gospel. I alluded to this danger in the previous chapter. But it needs further attention. The history of the Christian church is polluted with far too many times when we allowed the surrounding non-Christian culture to distort our message or alter our vocabulary. If we think we're immune to such theological contamination today, we're in more danger than we realize.

First, we must acknowledge the temptation to shrink back. Why else would Jesus warn his disciples against being ashamed of him and his words (see Mark 8:38)? And why would Paul emphatically declare, "I am not ashamed of the gospel" (Rom. 1:16) if there wasn't some level of that possibility? As commentator Douglas Moo remarks, "'The foolishness of the word of the cross' (1 Cor. 1:18) would make some degree of embarrassment about the gospel natural."[12] Do we really think Peter's denials stemmed solely from his unique internal struggles? Shouldn't we rather see them as warnings for all followers of a Savior who was himself rejected and mocked?

Second, we need to remember the offensive nature of our message. The gospel offends because it tells people they're incapable of self-salvation. Other religions flatter. The way of the cross crushes. We shouldn't be surprised when people feel the force of that message. Nor should we be shocked by internal temptations to soften the blow. We do want to "become all things to all people" (1 Cor. 9:22) but we must not allow them to write the script.

I remember participating in a panel of campus ministers at a conference sponsored by an "Institute for Conflict Analysis and Resolution." The hosts wanted to explore how universities could eliminate religious organizations' attempts to "proselytize." At one very awkward moment, the attention pointed my way when a questioner wondered why it was only Christians who caused "these problems" on campus. Before I could offer a defense, the Buddhist chaplain came to my rescue. He himself was raised in a Christian home and converted to Buddhism during his undergraduate days. "They can't help it," he began. "There's something unique to their message that bothers people. I can put up a million posters on campus inviting people to our meditation classes and nobody minds. But when Christians advertise their Bible studies or events, some people get all hot and bothered. I've seen it many times. You can't make that disappear." Without his spelling it out, people there seemed to connect his explanation with the fact that Jesus always bothered some people, and his followers might not be able to avoid the same response.

The inevitability of offense, unfortunately, causes some Christians to amp up the volume and intensify the anger. This may be just as bad as the tendency to clam up and say nothing. We must find ways to face the very possibility of offending and proclaim our message anyway—without sounding shrill or insulting. Praying for God to give us boldness in the face of fear and kindness in the midst of hostility must form the foundation of evangelistic efforts at every turn.

The Ultimate Antidote to Fear

I've heard some people offer "the fear of the Lord" as the solution to "the fear of man." I believe they are correct. But the way some have expressed that truth needs clarification. They warn, "Are you more fearful of what people will think of you or more afraid of what God will say when he sees you shrink back?" Replacing one fear with another still leaves us in fear. It also fails to grasp the significant differences between the two kinds of fear. The fear of man paralyzes. The fear of God transforms.

The Bible mentions "the fear of the Lord" many times. God weaves it as the unifying theme of the poetry books (Psalms, Proverbs, Job, Ecclesiastes, Song of Songs) and breathes it into the mouths of the prophets at key junctures. In the New Testament, *after* the resurrection, we're told that "the church . . . was strengthened. Living in the fear of the Lord and encouraged by the Holy Spirit, it increased in numbers" (Acts 9:31).

> As we grow gradually in love for God, who loves us limitlessly, our fear of people will be replaced with love for them.

There's far more to this topic than I can offer here. But I will say we need to live in the fear of the Lord just as the early church did. When we marvel at how holy God is, how perfect his ways are, how reasonable his wrath toward sin is, *and yet* how undeserved his saving, blood-bought grace is, we will bow in worship and awe. That process will remake us into different people. As we grow gradually in love for God, who loves us limitlessly, our fear of people will be replaced with love for them. The fear of the Lord will dissipate our fear of people.

Consider the sequence of rationale Paul outlined in Romans 1:16–17, the statement we've already considered about being ashamed of the gospel. Note in verse 16 Paul's reason why he's not ashamed: "I am not ashamed of the gospel, *because* it is the power of God that brings salvation to everyone who believes: first to the Jew, then to the Gentile" (emphasis mine). Paul contrasts any fear he had with the goodness of the good news. Our message is powerful, he mulls over. It's so powerful that it can save anyone, regardless of their religious background or level of religious accomplishment.

Paul then goes on in verse 17 to offer a reason for the gospel's power: "For in the gospel the righteousness of God is revealed—a righteousness that is by faith from first to last, just as it is written: 'The righteous will live by faith.'" The sequence of these rationales actually began back in verse 15: "I am so eager to preach the gospel" and certainly am not ashamed of it—for it is powerful because it's based on faith, not on works. The intensity of the sequence grows as Paul builds reason after reason.

We need to preach the gospel to ourselves, reminding ourselves of its uniqueness, power, and goodness. These reminders need to be more than mere rote recitations of memorized verses (although memorizing verses can provide the fuel for our meditations). They need to be extensive, thoughtful, worshipful ruminations that work their way deep into our doubts and fears. Paul models this well for us in these verses. We need to follow his lead and shine the light of the good news into the dark crevices of our fears. We will discover, to use Thomas Chalmers's insight, that this "new affection" has "expulsive power."[13]

Preaching the gospel to ourselves, mulling it over, and exploring its ramifications in our own lives does more than set us free from fear of others. It increases our love for them and emboldens us to tell them how it applies to their lives. It changes the very tone of our voice as we tell people how wonderful the gospel is. It shifts the weight of our presentations from "Here are the arguments that defeat your arguments" to "Here's something that is so good, you should embrace it." We don't just implore them, "You should believe this because it's true." We also imply, "You should believe this because it's good." (Note that we should do both! The gospel is both true and good.)

I wish this was an instantaneous change instead of a lifelong process, like flipping a switch instead of like kneading dough. Wouldn't it be great if we went from "I'm afraid to tell this person about Jesus" to "I'm afraid of nothing!" simply by reminding ourselves that God loves us and accepts us because Jesus died for us. That is the right sequence. I just think the pace of transformation occurs more slowly than we'd like.

On the Other Side of Fear

Of all the stories I heard when interviewing recent converts, few illustrated the value of courage in evangelism more than Edward's. He kept telling me about one particular person who dared to talk to him when everyone else avoided him. Granted, there were good reasons to steer clear. He described himself as "a hostile atheist" who "dropped out of college to be a meth addict—and to cook the stuff in a makeshift lab." His first two years in school grew incrementally in drug-induced stupors. At first, it was "just" alcohol and marijuana but, as the intellectual arguments in his philosophy classes pointed in nihilistic directions, he found fewer and fewer reasons to say no to cocaine, hallucinogens, and "really hard stuff." Eventually, meth took over his life, obliterating any possibility of going to classes.

That's how Edward ended up dropping out but staying nearby— homeless, "grungy and disgusting." He couldn't return home; his parents wouldn't let him do meth. But he couldn't stay in school either. One guy from his dorm, Len, would meet him on a bench near campus and answer questions about the meaning of life. Len shared how he had become a Christian and found hope, contrary to most of what he heard in class. Edward couldn't believe Len was so patient. He couldn't even fathom how Len came within ten feet of him—he hadn't bathed in weeks. He remembered a few specifics about Len that stood out: He made eye contact. He waited patiently for an answer whenever he asked a question. And he shared his own story of faith with a joy that didn't seem weird.

They met one last time right before Len graduated when he gave Edward a New Testament to read. Len was about to leave town to "go to seminary," something that sounded absolutely foreign. But Edward thanked him for the book and somehow hoped to see him again. Not long after Len left town, a fellow addict died from an overdose, scaring Edward into treatment. A local twelve-step program actually worked. "Sobriety was a miracle," he told me, and that budged him from hostile atheism to humble theism.

Now that he was off the drugs, Edward reenrolled in school. He also got a job in sales, which required him to travel on weekends. On one sales trip, he decided to visit Len because his seminary was nearby. He wondered if he might help him find answers to his remaining questions. The way he recounted the next part of his story still amazes me. He got on the plane (with the New Testament Len gave him) and made a list of questions to ask Len. "But by the time the plane landed, those objections were no longer objections." When he finally got together with Len, some of his first words were, "I guess your prayers have been answered."

I'm leaving out a lot of details, which might cause you to be skeptical, especially in light of the last chapter's cautions about false conversions. I asked Edward a lot of questions. So did Len. So did the church that hired him to be their missions pastor. In a rough neighborhood, he now shares his story on a regular basis—sometimes even in the midst of fear.

BRAINSTORMS: COMFORT

One of the biggest fears Christians face is knowing what to say about the problem of evil. People around us will suffer. We should count on it. And we should prepare ourselves to go beyond the trite clichés they'll hear from others. Perhaps more than any other situation, the problem of pain takes the most amount of forethought. Here are some suggestions for being a supportive voice in the midst of trouble:

- I heard you had a pretty tough week. I'm sorry to hear that. Please know that I'll be praying for you. Are there other ways I can help?
- Thanks for asking me that question about suffering. I've thought about that a lot and I still wrestle with it. But I think I might be able to help. Or at least we could discuss it, and maybe both of us will learn from each other. How does that sound?
- I'm so sorry to hear about your loss. I'd like to come to your father's funeral to support you. Can you tell me the details about when and where it will be?
- Some of my most helpful realizations came during the roughest

times. If you'd ever want to talk about those kinds of things, I'd be glad to listen.

- I get the idea your life has been full of major decisions lately. Want a take a break for a few minor decisions—like what to order off the menu for lunch? I'll buy.

CHAPTER 7

Kindly

Roger seemed to have it all—a steady girlfriend, a starting position on his high school's basketball team, and the title of student body president. He was tall, good looking, smart, and confident. But things weren't as good as they seemed. One day when his girlfriend called his house (long before the days of cell phones), his mother told her, "Oh, Roger doesn't live here anymore." Indeed, Roger didn't live with his mother because she told him, "You *can't* live here anymore." Roger's father had left his mother for another woman when Roger was only nine years old. His mother's alcoholism and drug problems had taken over her life, and now she didn't want her son around her anymore.

So Roger lived in his truck. He'd grab a shower at a friend's house every now and then and occasionally crash on someone's couch, but for more than a month, he was quite literally homeless. Briefly, Roger considered moving several hours away to live again with his father. But he decided not to when his father responded to his son's request with, "Well . . . you need to know I smoke a lot of marijuana, and that's not going to change if you move in here."

When the parents of Roger's girlfriend found all this out, they invited him to move in with their family. It was a small house with only enough bedrooms for their family of five, but they turned their den—"the largest and nicest room in the house"—into "Roger's room." You might think it unwise for them to have their daughter's boyfriend live under the same roof, but they thought it was worth the risk. He stayed with them for over a year before going off to college. "They bought me a whole new wardrobe and loved me well."

He remembers that his girlfriend's only brother thought this was the best news in the world. Before then, the family ate extremely healthily, almost vegan. But when they saw that Roger had not eaten well for several months ("I was like six foot five, one hundred fifty pounds, gray, and looked sickly and malnourished"), they fattened him up (along with the girlfriend's brother!) with cheeseburgers, Pop-Tarts, Oreos, and ice cream galore.

Roger was not a Christian. Like many others, being abandoned by an earthly father made him cast doubt on anything good about a heavenly one. "I grew up in the Christ-haunted South that was full of hypocrisy," he told me, and "I became an ardent agnostic." By the time he reached his junior year in high school, he had spent a lot of time in libraries, reading and becoming convinced by existentialist philosophers like Camus and Sartre. When he posed intellectually challenging questions to his churchgoing friends, they couldn't answer. He concluded Christianity was for the intellectually uninformed and people who just didn't think too deeply.

His new "family" (that's how he speaks of them now—over twenty years later) were Christians and invited him to join them at church. They didn't require it, but he figured that would be a polite thing to do, considering all the nice things they were doing for him. At that church, he encountered a Christianity that differed dramatically from the shallow models he'd seen up until then. He recounted with a tear in his eye that they "added intellectual credibility" to their expressions of faith. "They were patient with my many questions," and they pointed him to intellectually respectable writers like C. S. Lewis. In conversations with individual people and through the pastor's sermons, he heard this recurring theme: "Everything in this world will let you down. Nothing will ever be enough. But if you know Christ, he'll be enough. He'll add meaning to everything else."

As Roger recounted his story to me, he wove together two strands he said couldn't be separated: intellectual depth and gracious character. "They lived in a way that added credibility to the statements they made. I kept wondering, 'Why are you being so nice to me?'" and they kept pointing to how "nice" God had been to them. They weren't perfect people. In fact, at the very end of our conversation, Roger told me, "In the most loving way, it's right for me to say, they [his new parents] were some of the most unremarkable people you'll ever meet. They're never going to stand out in a crowd. They're never going to show up on some kind of list. But they're incredibly faithful and have been used to change many people's lives—not just mine."

When I asked Roger about the shift from unbelief to belief, he told me, "After living with them for almost a year, there was this moment when I thought, 'I believe this is true.' I surrendered to God's pursuit of me." He sketched out this scenario: He was preparing to take his girlfriend to the senior prom. For this special event, a family friend lent him "this really nice Porsche." He was driving on a beautiful highway through breathtaking scenery and thought, "If everything goes right, this is as good as it's gonna get. I could someday drive a car like this, and this could be my life." He paused and added, "But then I thought, 'Is that it? Is that all there is?' It all came together for me at that moment. Soon after that, I told my family, 'Yeah, I believe.'"

> Arguing whether words or deeds are
> more important for evangelism is like
> debating over which wing of an airplane
> is more important for successful flight.

The stability of a new home and family had its effect on Roger's academic life as well. His grades improved enough for him to get accepted at several colleges. His new family drove him to numerous campus tours and made sacrifices "like I was just part of their family." Indeed, years later, when he and his girlfriend broke up, her parents reiterated, "This is your home. You can come back here any time." He did return there many times. He still does, decades later—with his wife and their two kids, who are named after his "adopted parents."

Words and Deeds, Logic and Life

I repeat the important duality Roger expressed in his story: intellectual depth and gracious character. The gospel is both true and good. We evangelize with both answers and affection. And we must not pit these two dimensions of outreach against each other. Arguing whether words or deeds are more important for evangelism is like debating over which wing of an airplane is more important for successful flight.

Note the blend of both ingredients in Colossians 4:3–6. "Pray for us, too, that God may open a door for our message, so that we may proclaim the mystery of Christ, for which I am in chains. Pray that I may proclaim it clearly, as I should. Be wise in the way you act toward outsiders; make the most of every opportunity. Let your conversation be always full of grace, seasoned with salt, so that you may know how to answer everyone."

There's plenty about words in this passage ("message," "proclaim," "clearly," "conversation," "answer"). But "the way you act" sits right in the middle of this endorsement of verbal proclamation. Both our vocabulary and our demeanor should reflect the goodness of our message. We need to convey our message with both words and deeds, truth and goodness, things we say and things we do. And let's not forget that kindness is part of the fruit of the Spirit (Gal. 5:22).

Conversation that is both "full of grace and seasoned with salt" means that our speech is both attractive and stimulating, inviting and surprising, good news and challenging probes. Several of the people I interviewed told me the Christians they met were kind to them but also shook up their thinking. They offered expressions like "We're really glad you're here," but also posed questions like "What has convinced you of your current beliefs?"

Tony told me he needed both the grace and the salt. "On the outside, everything was great for me. But on the inside, I was so unhappy with my life. I was unsure of my purpose. I never hurt myself, but I contemplated suicide a lot. I would sometimes sit and be like, 'I don't know. Maybe I'll end my life today.'"

He met a group of Christians during his freshman year in college who invited him into their sphere of friendship. They also challenged him to think deeply about the Bible. Sitting in weekly Bible studies brought him answers and acceptance. But his lifestyle took longer to change. During one Christmas break he had "two bad nights in a row." When I asked him what that meant, he said he had so much alcohol that he blacked out twice in a row. It was the in-a-row part that scared him. I asked if he had ever blacked out before. "Oh, yeah. Lots of times. But never two nights back-to-back." He recounted all this with very little emotion.

When he got back to campus, he reconnected with his Bible study friends and dug in deeply to study and ask tough questions. Up until then, "I always thought that God had bigger problems to deal with than me being unhappy, so I didn't feel the need to call on him or talk to him." All that changed after the dual blackouts. Many in-depth conversations with friends, hours of reading the Scriptures, and lots of reflections on how the gospel makes people radiant, loved, and accepted moved him from despair to praise.

Peter tells us to defend our faith "with gentleness and respect." I wonder if part of that is because we never know the dramas going on behind people's faces. Might they have been wondering, "Maybe I'll end my life today"? Our grace and salt might just help them consider something far better.

The Kindness of Conversation

Colossians 4:6 mentions "conversation." It's a general term that means speech of all kind—about the gospel, the weather, or any-thing at all. I'm convinced that conversations do some things that presentations don't. The two-way, back-and-forth nature of a dia-logue paves the way for reception of ideas in ways that one-way com-munication does not.

Conversations might even be more helpful than books (something an author is loath to admit). I will add this clarification: I'm not disparaging preaching or one-way proclamation through sermons, lectures, books, or informal talks. They are tremendously powerful and emphatically endorsed in Scripture. But they work in different ways than conversations. We need both.

People who study the nature of conversation have some pretty lofty things to say about it. Best-selling author and linguistics scholar Deborah Tannen claims, "A perfectly tuned conversation is a vision of sanity—a ratification of one's way of being human and one's place in the world."[1] Several shelves in large bookstores are dedicated to help people improve their relationships, careers, self-esteem, and even physical well-being through meaningful conversation. They promise that conversation can change our lives, change how we see the world, and even change the world.[2]

MIT professor Sherry Turkle and author of *Reclaiming Conversation*, while warning of the dangers technology poses to conversation, affirms that "face-to-face conversation is the most human—and humanizing—thing we do. Fully present to one another, we learn to listen. It's where we develop the capacity for empathy. It's where we experience the joy of being heard, of being understood. And conversation advances self-reflection, the conversations with ourselves that are the cornerstones of early development and continue throughout life."[3] Turkle is concerned about how cell phones and other technology harm our face-to-face interactions. But she's not pessimistic. As the title of her book suggests, we can reclaim conversation.

If becoming a Christian involves more than just agreeing with certain propositions (and it most certainly does), I believe the process of conversation can serve as a helpful tool in evangelism. If "belief in God is more like belief in a person than belief in a scientific theory,"[4] then conversations can introduce people to the personal, communicative, knowable God who made them in his image.

Samuel told me that many "incredibly lengthy conversations" with three different people were the most important parts of his journey to faith. All three showed great patience with his many questions and allowed him to process things gradually and slowly. "It was a lot to eat in just one sitting," he told me, using a metaphor he repeated several times. It was over time, through numerous conversations, that he observed both "logical coherence" in what his friends were saying and "a true working out of their beliefs" in their lives.

One friend was "an amazing shoulder to cry on" when Samuel went through a painful breakup. Another friend provided "either the answer or the promise of an answer that would prove to be satisfying." The third friend disagreed with Samuel with a graciousness that impressed him. "I had never met anyone who was both confident in what he knew to be true but also humble about himself." On several occasions, when Samuel verbally processed something that was clearly contrary to biblical teaching, this friend would pause and softly say, "I don't think so."

Samuel told me several times, "I think I'm the kind of person who needs to process things out loud." His statement confirmed his theory. But I wonder if both internal and external processors need time or incremental installments to wrestle with the concept that God is both holy and loving. That's the theological conundrum that tripped Samuel up for months and required repeated conversations with friends who were both patient and stalwart.

Include social skills and communication technique training as part of discipleship efforts. Let's help Christians converse about the weather as well as talking about eternity.

Research supports my theory. Seminary professor Gary L. McIntosh conducted extensive study on how people are actually coming to faith today. He found that, unlike earlier times when people responded to a methodology (such as a booklet or a preconstructed presentation), people now come to faith mostly "through natural conversations . . . with a family member or friend or staff member."[5] At a bare minimum, this means we should include social skills and communication technique training as part of discipleship efforts. Let's help Christians converse about the weather as well as talking about eternity.

Conversation and Conversion

Part of the reason that conversation helps in evangelism stems from the nature of Christian conversion. When people become Christians, they do more than just change their thinking. They turn, trust, repent, and receive. God makes them new creatures, raises them from the dead, and adopts them. There's far more going on here than a change in opinion. Conversations can move multifaceted people in diverse ways through a complex conversion process.

When I researched what social scientists have to say about the nature of conversion, I found they tended to homogenize a wide range of conversions to see what they had in common. This was helpful up to a point. But it also had tremendous limitations. Comparing the experience of a Jewish person becoming a Buddhist to a religious person becoming an atheist does not help us think precisely about the nature of distinct conversions. Seeing similarities in different conversions has some merit, but it fails to challenge a prevailing view of secularism that says all religions are the same.

All religions are *not* the same, and, correspondingly, all conversions are not the same. Some people describe their conversions to Eastern mysticism as "enlightenment." Others use terms like "understanding," "discovery," "writing my own destiny," or "making myself into the person I determined to be." The Scriptures describe the process of Christian conversion differently, with words like *repentance* and *becoming undone*.

Some of the studies I read looked beyond religious experiences to find common denominators with other kinds of conversions. They wondered how switching from one religion to another, or from a religious perspective to a secular one, compared to changing political parties, or adopting changes in diet, or becoming athletically active. At the risk of belaboring the point, converting to Christianity differs radically from converting to vegetarianism.

The Bible describes the act of becoming a Christian as far more involved, complex, and eternally significant than other life changes. That's why it might take some people longer than just a few minutes to receive it. By the way, consider that word *receive*. When John used it in his gospel's introduction, he meant far more than intellectual assent. People who "did not receive him" (John 1:11) did more than disagree with Jesus. They did not recognize him and later they conspired to kill him. Those who "did receive him" did more than just understand things Jesus said; they "[became] children of God" (v. 12).

Lengthy, multiple-installment, emotion-saturated conversations can propel the conversion process forward in powerful ways—if we ask God for patience and wisdom as partners in that process.

Varieties of Kindness

Kindness comes in numerous forms. Weaving together works and words looks different in different settings, for different people, or at different times. I'll offer four possible varieties of kindness, with the hope that these will spark ideas for dozens more.

Kindness as Empathy

Kindness can be expressed as empathy, echoing someone's feelings, affirming their responses, validating their experiences. It can be expressed through sharing a similar experience you once had as you journeyed toward saving faith. It can be expressed as concisely as "That makes sense" or "I can see that." We can also convey empathy toward an outsider by asking questions that show we want to hear more from them. "Please help me understand that. Can you tell me a little more?" shows people you respect them and can relate to their struggle to understand the gospel.

Far too often, our words, faces, and posture say, "How can you not understand this? It's so simple!" Should we be surprised if people may not engage with us when we repel them early in the process?

Kindness as Patience

For those of us who have been Christians a long time, it might be difficult to remember how gradually we moved toward faith. We might not recall how tough certain concepts were for us to understand. And we might forget completely all the intermediate steps of semi-belief we took before arriving at saving faith.

As we converse with some nonbelievers, we need to ask God for patience as we deliver our message with pauses for reflection (theirs) and considerate repetitions (ours). One way to frame this is to see our task through three lenses:

- What is the question (or questions) my friend is asking?
- What is the answer (from Scripture, and with support from other sources)?
- How shall I deliver the answer?

For example, if your conversation partner asks the age-old question about evil and suffering, we should first clarify which variety of that problem they find most troubling. When someone says, "How can you believe in a God who allows so much evil and suffering?" they could be expressing many different things.

Some people might want an intellectual, philosophical investigation, though I have found them to be in the minority. Some feel extreme pain from a personal tragedy or the recent death of a loved one. Others want to believe in God, but they find themselves needing a sympathetic affirmation to do so. Others are angry at God. Many other varieties of doubt lurk behind the initial asking of the question.

Which answer we deliver depends on which question they're asking. A philosophical treatise about the nature of evil sounds irrelevant or even cruel to someone who struggles with the reality of physical pain on a daily basis. On the other hand, a statement of "I know how you feel" seems completely inappropriate to someone asking a genuine intellectual question. It takes discernment and thought before spouting words you've heard at a recent apologetics seminar.

We may choose to deliver our answer incrementally. That could sound like this:

1. *An acknowledgement that the question is reasonable.* "Yes, that trips up a lot of people, and I think I understand why. There really are a lot of disturbing things going on in our world. I actually struggle with this question myself some of the time."
2. *An encouragement to pursue the issue.* "I hope you won't just ask this question and stay stuck. I don't think that's the best way to handle it. I do think there are some helpful ways people have dealt with this. I know I've been helped by thinking a lot about suffering."
3. *A sketch of some different options for answers.* "For a while I considered the atheistic response to suffering—stuff just happens. That didn't really help me. There's too much good in the world to settle for the theory that life is absurd. I also dug into other worldviews that simply said that suffering is just a part of life that we need to embrace. That didn't work for me either."
4. *A brief mention of the Christian answer.* "The Christian understanding about suffering has helped me the most. It still holds some frustrations for me. But I've found a lot of comfort and hope in it. Can I tell you about that?"
5. *An expansion on the Christian answer.* "Christianity has a framework to understand the suffering in the world. We believe the world is fallen and all sorts of problems result. But we also believe in redemption because Jesus died to pay for the very things that cause so much suffering. This gives us hope that he's begun a process of setting things right. But we're in the middle of that process, and sometimes that's very, very difficult. Is this making sense?"

> Kindness can be conveyed through
> the word *no* as well as *yes.*

Obviously, there's so much more that could and needs to be said. But I'm hoping you catch the flavor of expressing kindness patiently instead of unloading a dump truck full of answers bluntly. Ironically, sometimes the willingness to move slowly actually speeds along the process!

Kindness as Constructive Disagreement

Kindness can be conveyed through the word *no* as well as *yes*. We must disagree with some, perhaps many, of the things non-Christians believe and say. But we must find ways to do so constructively. This is no easy task. In our world today, people disagree sarcastically, dismissively, angrily, loudly, and harshly. They do so through indirect communication like Facebook and Twitter instead of through face-to-face conversation. The climate into which we speak resembles a cesspool. Many Christians simply choose to withdraw and say nothing.

But we must find ways to "speak the truth in love" (Eph. 4:15) and express disagreement with ideas without disapproval of the people who express them. Many of the people I interviewed told me how struck they were when a friend dared to challenge their beliefs. Just hearing "I disagree" impressed them, while gently disorienting them.

In some cases, disagreement needs preparation, like entering your password on your phone before opening an app. We need to pave the way toward saying something that counters what has just been said. For instance:

- "If I'm understanding you, I think I disagree. Can we explore this?"
- "It sounds like you'd like to discuss this. Am I right? You probably can tell that we hold different perspectives on this."
- "I know our world is pretty divided right now. And it usually sounds harsh. But I wonder if we can be different when we talk about religion. I'd like to try. Would you?"

Then, once we've prepared the way, disagreement can take many forms—but they all need to be gentle, kind, respectful, with lower volume and greater efforts to clarify. And if you have an advanced competency in sarcasm, you need to turn that off.

Kindness as constructive disagreement might sound like this:

- "I think I understand what you're saying. And I'm pretty sure I disagree. Here are a few reasons why I've come to this position."
- "What you've just said makes a lot of sense. I can see how you've come to that view. Here's another perspective."
- "I've asked you to read that book about Christianity that I gave you. If you've got something you'd like me to read to better grasp your faith perspective, I'd be glad to read it. How does that sound?"

For some people, the content of the disagreement is less compelling than the tone of the discussion. One friend once told me, "In my family, we all yelled. It didn't matter what we were talking about. We all sounded mad. When I first met Christians who took their faith seriously, I was more impressed with *how* they said things than with *what* they actually said. It was like eavesdropping on a foreign language, with a very nice tone and a sweet flavor."

Kindness as Contrast

Sometimes kindness shines in dramatic contrast to the darkness of surrounding cultures. Christians today have much to learn from our forebears. Several historians have documented how early Christians voiced radical views on moral issues that, while bringing them persecution, also attracted many to the gospel.[6]

They took unpopular stands against abortion, infanticide, and divorce and faced social and political rejection as a result. But the same issue that drew mockery also drew converts. People were drawn to a God of infinite love, one that differed entirely from the popular gods of early Rome. New Testament scholar Larry Hurtado concludes, "It was incredible to some, and, I suggest, powerfully winsome for some others."[7]

Here's a recent expression of kindness as contrast. A local pro-life ministry hosts an eight-week Bible study for women who choose to bring their babies to term. Some of them have been abused or raped. Most have been pressured to have an abortion, being told it's the only solution to their unwanted pregnancy. Some have been warned to stay away from Christians "because they'll just condemn you."

At the end of the eight-week Bible study, the organization hosts a joint baby shower. In a large house, dozens of women gather to celebrate life. After a time of eating an elaborate brunch, the group divides into various rooms in the house—with one pregnant woman and six or seven Christian "supporters" at each mini-shower. In addition to the women who have led the Bible study, new friends purchase and present car seats, strollers, baby clothes, toys, and mountains of diapers. They've done this enough times to know they should stock each location in the house with several boxes of tissues. Tears flow along with the kindness and grace.

A Kindness-Starved World

There's a genre of communication we need to take seriously as expressions of cultural priorities: commencement speeches. In recent years, authors, entertainers, politicians, and other guest speakers have delivered memorable addresses that went viral on YouTube. In some cases, they were then published as concise, somewhat over-priced, hardback books that became best sellers. Their topics tell us a great deal about what people value highly and long for deeply.

In 2013, at Syracuse University's graduation, author and professor George Saunders delivered a talk about kindness that reveals a hunger we should recognize and respond to. He began lightheartedly with a series of recollections of things he probably should have regretted but didn't. He then delivered the speech's thesis statement: "What I regret most in my life are failures of kindness." He added, "As a goal in life, you could do worse than: Try to be kinder."[8]

He admitted this is no easy task. Philosophically, he offered a threefold hypothesis on why we are not kind. First, "We're central to the universe (that is, our personal story is the main and most interesting story, the *only* story, really)." Second, "We're separate from the universe." And third, "We're permanent (death is real . . . for you, but not for me)."

Saunders then offered some suggestions for how we might overcome obstacles to become kinder. "Education is good; immersing ourselves in a work of art, good; prayer is good; meditation's good; a frank talk with a dear friend" and several other practical, reasonable ideas were all pronounced "good."

At the end of his speech, he dug a bit deeper into the problem. "There's a confusion in each of us, a sickness, really: selfishness. But there's a cure." His analysis of the problem resonates with Scripture, but his solution falls woefully short: "To the extent that you can, err in the direction of kindness."

As is the case with so many thoughtful searches for truth in the culture around us, we can critique and ridicule or we can affirm and expand. We could pronounce a loud "no" to Saunders's suggestions for improving ourselves and our world. Or we can offer a kind "yes, *and* . . ." We can point people to the greatest act of kindness ever accomplished and show how it can make us kinder toward each other. We can agree with his analysis of our problem and add, "I think it's even worse than just selfishness." We can point to a solution far better than just our best efforts to "err in the direction of kindness."

Consider the word *kindness* tucked into Paul's restatement of the gospel to Titus:

> At one time we too were foolish, disobedient, deceived and enslaved by all kinds of passions and pleasures. We lived in malice and envy, being hated and hating one another. But when the kindness and love of God our Savior appeared, he saved us, not because of righteous things we had done, but because of his mercy. He saved us through the washing of rebirth and renewal by the Holy Spirit, whom he poured out on us generously through Jesus Christ our Savior, so that, having been justified by his grace, we might become heirs having the hope of eternal life. (Titus 3:3–7)

Divine Models of Kindness

In conclusion, consider the following kind invitation God makes through the prophet Isaiah. Many others could be found in Isaiah and other prophets as well. Catch the tone of God's gracious, hope-inspiring words:

> Come, all you who are thirsty,
>   come to the waters;
> and you who have no money,
>   come, buy and eat!
> Come, buy wine and milk
>   without money and without cost.
> Why spend money on what is not bread,
>   and your labor on what does not satisfy?
> Listen, listen to me, and eat what is good,
>   and you will delight in the richest of fare. (Isa. 55:1–2)

Do you feel the emotion behind these words? Do you sense an imploring in the repetition of the words *come* and *listen*? Do you catch the seeming incongruity between "buying" and "having no money"? How can someone buy something if they have no money? Note that the prophet does not say, "You who have no money, come and take. It doesn't cost anything!" Our salvation is amazingly costly.

> We seek to reach people who
> are starving for kindness.

As Old Testament scholar Alec Motyer points out, "Someone—in context, by implication, the Servant in his saving efficacy [see Isa. 52:13–53:12]—has paid the purchase price."[9] That's how people without money can receive what has been purchased for them. And, Oh![10] What a bountiful purchase it is—water for the thirsty, wine and milk (costly luxuries in Isaiah's day) for the hungry, and goodness that delights our soul in ways that nothing else can satisfy.

We seek to reach people who are starving for kindness. We can "do worse than err on the side" of announcing the good news of "the richest of fare" with gospel-saturated kindness.

BRAINSTORMS: KINDNESSES

I've already suggested ways we can express kindness or empathy or constructive disagreement through words. So I won't add more to the list of things we can say. Instead, here are some questions we can ask ourselves as we consider next steps to take in outreach.

- Have I already begun conversations that start with the mundane? (Where are you from? What do you do for a living? How's your family?) If not, how can I take the first step?
- If I have started the conversation, what might be some next steps to deepen it?
- What are some nonverbal actions I can take that might build bridges?
- Does the person appear to have some needs I could meet? Is he going through a tough time? Does she live alone and could use some companionship?
- What spiritual gifts do I have that could be used in outreach? If I don't have the gift of evangelism, how might my gift of helps, or mercy, or teaching, or encouragement, or giving, or some other gift (see Rom. 12:3–8, for example) be used as part of the body of Christ in outreach?

CHAPTER 8

Prayerfully

Carlos told me his mother was a godly woman who prayed a lot. As I listened to his story, I couldn't imagine his mother not spending hours on her knees. By the time Carlos reached his senior year in high school, he experienced what he called "a descending lifestyle." You can imagine the ingredients—drugs, alcohol, peer pressure, suicidal thoughts—but that would only account for part of the picture. An intellectual curiosity and a sharp mind plunged him into a depressing cycle of reading atheistic rants and "watching a lot of philosophical videos and things about religion—both good and bad."

The unique twist for Carlos's story was the rags-to-riches drama of his immigrant family coming to America and struggling to survive. For a time he, along with his father and mother, were homeless, living in a car "some people just gave us." Some other kind people, Christians from a nearby church, eventually gave them a place to live, helped his parents find jobs, and even gave them a computer.

One would hope that such a story would turn to the happy ending at that point. Kindness leads to conversion, right? Didn't I just imply that in the previous chapter? But such straight lines of cause and effect are rare in conversion narratives. For Carlos, the spiritual plummet began with the rise in economic stability. The luxury of a roof over their heads and a computer in his bedroom opened the ways for Carlos to descend.

Did Carlos's mother pray for him? I'm pretty sure she did. I didn't interview her but Carlos did say he saw her on her knees several times, often in tears. Can we connect those prayers to his turnaround? Did her intercessions spark his reading of Christian books, watching online videos that featured R. C. Sproul, Ravi Zacharias, John Lennox, and other apologists? Did his mother's attitude toward God change Carlos's attitude toward Christians—from "annoyance" to "intrigue"?

Encouragement from Scripture

Prayer may always mystify us. How our requests affect God's actions falls outside anyone's intellectual capabilities. But we are on solid biblical ground to assume that prayer and evangelism are linked. I have pointed to Colossians 4:2–6 several times as an underpinning for this book. The passage also supports the notion that intercession and outreach weave together. Consider that Paul asks for prayer for an open door for outreach after exhorting the Colossians to "devote [themselves] to prayer, being watchful and thankful" (v. 2).

> Even the most stalwart of prayer warriors
> may get tempted to lose heart. Why
> else would . . . Jesus have told us the
> parable of the persistent widow?

While this passage may convince us that prayer and evangelism are inseparable, even the most stalwart of prayer warriors may get tempted to lose heart. Why else would Paul tell us to "devote" ourselves to the task, and why else would Jesus have told us the parable of the persistent widow? The text tells us why—so that we would "always pray and not give up" (Luke 18:1). If there's one thing I've learned about prayer, it's that it's easy to quit. Talking to an invisible God about things we can rarely measure sets us up for diminished enthusiasm. And this is especially true when it comes to praying for unsaved people to come to faith. I find it encouraging that Paul told the Colossians, "Epaphras . . . is always wrestling in prayer for you" (Col. 4:12). Wrestling! Now there's an image that captures the realities of intercession.

Some have questioned whether we should pray for the salvation of nonbelievers. They claim that the prayers recorded for us in the New Testament are for Christians. Paul prayed for believers to grow, not for outsiders to get saved, they argue. But they fail to take into account all the data. To be sure, most of Paul's prayers focus on the believers to whom he writes. But he also prayed for the salvation of nonbelievers. He told the church in Rome that his "heart's desire and prayer to God for the Israelites is that they may be saved" (Rom. 10:1). And when Agrippa asked Paul if he thought his preaching would actually persuade him to become a Christian "in such a short time," Paul replied, "Short time or long—I pray to God that not only you but all who are listening to me today may become what I am." Then, almost as comic relief, he added, "except for these chains" (Acts 26:28–29).

I conclude that we do have biblical warrant for praying for unsaved people's salvation. And that takes devotion. We'd much rather they respond in a "short time" rather than a "long time." To help us remain devoted to prayer, Paul offers two suggestions: watchfulness and thankfulness. After we pray, we watch and see how God may be orchestrating his dynamic answer to prayer. And when we see answers, we should take note. That's why many people have found it helpful to keep a written prayer journal, complete with dates of when prayers were first offered and dates for when God answered. The blank lines on the pages, where we're still waiting for answers, will be surrounded by inked evidence to help us persevere.

We should also consider another problem that has tempted some Christians to lose heart in prayer: trying to make sense of it all. If we insist on understanding how God works in answering prayer, when he in fact already knows everything and causes all things to conform to his will, we will find ourselves in the quagmire of prayerlessness.

Consider what New Testament scholar D. A. Carson has to offer about this puzzle:

> If you believe that God "elects" or chooses some people
> for eternal life, and does not choose others, you might be

tempted to conclude that there is no point praying for the
lost. The elect will infallibly be saved: why bother praying
for them? . . . If on the other hand you think that God has
done all he can to save the lost, and now it all depends on
their free will, why ask God to save them? He has already
done his bit; there's very little else for him to do. Just get out
there and preach the gospel. . . . You can really hurt your
head thinking about this sort of thing.[1]

Carson wrote an entire doctoral dissertation about the relationship between divine sovereignty and human responsibility.[2] If *he*'s
admitting the possibility of a headache from this kind of theological reflection, I'm willing to stop demanding total comprehension
before getting on my knees. He concludes: "The slightly ingenuous
but enthusiastic believer may have more experience at prayer than
the theologian who thinks a lot about prayer."[3]

Encouragement from Spectacular History

In addition to looking to Scripture, we can glance at the past. God
has worked in spectacular ways many times in the history of his
people. And prayer has played a significant part. Hearing these historical highpoints can motivate us to pray diligently and echo Psalm
85:6: "Will you not revive us again, that your people may rejoice in
you?" Some may be reluctant to sign on to the sweeping statement
of pastor and missionary A. T. Pierson, who declared, "There has
never been a spiritual awakening in any country or locality that did
not begin in united prayer."[4] But even if we add numerous caveats,
we cannot deny the biblical teaching on the efficacy of prayer and
the examples from history of God's choice to respond to prayer in
dramatic ways.

For several reasons (all of them bad), many Christians have heard
very little about revivals. Perhaps we recoil at the mental image of
emotion-manipulating camp meetings that claim more of God's
blessing than they should. Or perhaps we feel squeamish with the
notion of telling God when and how we want him to act. I share

these concerns. But God's word reiterates his will that we ask, seek, and knock (Matt. 7:7), not lose heart in prayer (Luke 18:1), and that we should "pray continually" (1 Thess. 5:17). What risks do we really face if we implore our sovereign God to draw unsaved people to himself, pour out his spirit of revival in our day, and advance his kingdom in dramatic, unprecedented ways? Indeed, could it be said that we "do not have because [we] do not ask God" (James 4:2)?

People who have studied revivals—genuine outpourings of God's power—exhort us to join them in their enthusiasm. Old Testament scholar Walter Kaiser urges us to begin with "examining the great revivals of the Bible."[5] Second Chronicles, for example, is a book totally crafted around the "central organizing motif" of revival.[6] Studying Old Testament revivals is contagious, insists Kaiser,[7] and will make us fervent in prayer for the evangelization of the nations.

Martyn Lloyd-Jones urged his church and readers of his important work, *Revival*, to study Scripture's teaching about revivals and history's examples of them. To fail to do so will leave us complacent and willing to settle for mediocre outreach and anemic preaching. Some, he bemoans, "have excluded revival altogether from their thinking and from their doctrine of the Holy Spirit."[8]

Collin Hansen and John Woodbridge, in their essential book, *A God-Sized Vision: Revival Stories That Stretch and Stir*, warn us, "Our problem today may be worse than mere forgetfulness. We've never even heard many of the revival stories that buoyed the faith of Lloyd-Jones. They've been lost."[9]

Perhaps no one has done as much to champion these stories than J. Edwin Orr, a first-rate scholar and seminary professor who wrote thousands of pages (over forty published books) to bring stories of revival to light. He used the phrase from Acts 3:19, "times of refreshing" to describe the works God has done throughout history. He elaborated, "The outpouring of the Spirit effects the reviving of the Church, the awakening of the masses, and the movement of uninstructed peoples towards the Christian faith; the revived Church, by many or by few, is moved to engage in evangelism, in teaching, and in social action."[10]

Church historian Richard Lovelace documented ways prayer has paved the way for expanded evangelism and spiritual renewal of churches. His research shows these "times of refreshing" were not just unusual emotional displays but a deepening of the church through "spiritual revitalization combined with doctrinal and structural reformation."[11]

Consider just two stories from our history that spark prayer for God to work powerfully—one amazing, the other amusing. America experienced "the closest thing to a truly national revival in [its] history"[12] in 1857–58. It began with extraordinary prayer and resulted in spectacular conversion growth of churches. J. Edwin Orr wrote an entire book about it, boldly titled *The Event of the Century*. As Hansen and Woodbridge describe, "Every Protestant denomination was caught up in its wake. . . . Between 1856 and 1859, Protestant denominations added 474,000 members."[13]

Often referred to as the "Prayer Meeting or Businessmen's Revival," it began when Jeremiah Lanphier (someone we know little about) invited businessmen to pray during a lunch hour he hoped to hold weekly. We do know that Lanphier spent a lot of time evangelizing people who lived around his church in Manhattan. Might we surmise that witnessing motivates us to pray? What could drive us to our knees more than evangelism—no matter how "successful" we might be?

The first prayer meeting seemed to lack evidence of divine blessing. No one showed up to join Lanphier for the first half hour. Eventually, six men arrived. But the next week, twenty came. Less than a month later, the average attendance grew to more than thirty, requiring them to move to a larger room. In less than two months, the attendance exploded to more than two hundred, attracting the attention of the secular news media of the day. Before long, other prayer meetings sprang up around the city and in other cities as well. Philadelphia's prayer meetings swelled to more than three thousand less than six months after Lanphier's first gathering. In a relatively short time, more than ten thousand people were gathering for prayer *every day*! Horace Greeley's *New York Tribune* even published a special revival issue. (Can you imagine hearing about something like this today from CNN?)

I encourage you to read Hansen and Woodbridge's stirring account of this seldom-told story. If that only whets your appetite, dig into Orr's three-hundred-plus-page retelling. You'll see that prayer was only the beginning. Hundreds of people sensed God's call to missionary and pastoral ministry during these meetings. Church worship services drew unsaved people by the scores. New converts were baptized in unprecedented numbers. And college campuses around the country erupted in revival.

The more you hear of this extraordinary moment, the less you'll think Orr overstated the title of his book. Better still, you'll be motivated to pray for God to work in similar ways in our world today. One friend told me he prays for spiritual "awakening" every morning when he wakes up. His own rising prompts him to ask God to rouse our world from its spiritual slumber.

> Just as prayer leads to conversions,
> so conversions lead to individual
> and societal change.

The second story demonstrates that just as prayer leads to conversions, so conversions lead to individual and societal change. God's saving work of rebirth is only the beginning of his transformational work of sanctification.

Fifty years after "the event of the century," another wave of revival broke out in Wales. Orr documents the effects of thousands of individual conversions in his book *The Flaming Tongue*. "Cases of drunkenness in Wales exceeded twenty thousand a year before the Revival but had dropped 33% in the three years following the movement. . . . Long standing debts were paid, and stolen goods returned."[14]

My favorite anecdote is about a slowdown in coal production because of the revival. That sounds odd, doesn't it? Orr recounts:

The life of the coal pits was transformed. Not only did workers and management engage in prayer meetings on the com-
pany's time which was being put to such good use in the
ordinary hours of activity, but the pits themselves showed
silent indicators of the new spirit—with texts chalked upon
ventilating doors for all to see who passed that way.

Cursing and profanity were so diminished that several
slowdowns were reported in the coal mines, for so many
men gave up using foul language that the pit ponies dragging
the coal trucks in the mine tunnels did not understand what
was being said to them and stood still, confused.[15]

Encouragement from the Less Than Spectacular

Hearing about revivals can indeed stretch and stir and motivate us to
pray for our evangelistic efforts. But it might also discourage some
of us. Anything short of earthshaking, dramatic, crowd-swelling
revival might make us wonder if we're making any impact at all.
Things might seem so bad at this current moment in time that we
could feel swept away by tidal waves of secularism, skepticism, and
spiritual apathy.

> Contrary to the seeming prevalence of
> secularism, people may be very interested in
> religion today and quite open to converting.

But a closer look at our current situation could bolster our devotion to prayer and jumpstart our boldness in outreach. Historian
Lincoln Mullen says, "Americans . . . change their religions—a lot."
Some "change religious traditions more than once." He relies on a
2009 Pew Research Center report that shows "46 percent of Americans have changed their religious affiliation from the faith in which
they had been raised as children."[16]

In an interview with Mullen, Emma Green, a staff writer for *The*

Atlantic (whose editors boldly titled the interview "Convert Nation"), offered, "There's a myth out there about American religion which goes something like this: We have reached a crisis point in religious affiliation. Everyone is running away from traditional religious observance, and religion is going to die. Your book significantly undermines that myth."[17]

Mullen affirmed her point. Contrary to the seeming prevalence of secularism, people may be very interested in religion today and quite open to converting. Mullen highlights the uniquely American nature of this openness. "Compared to most of Europe, the United States is famously religious."[18] He says this is because "the prevalence of religion as choice instead of religion as inheritance is distinctly (though not uniquely) American."[19]

I make much of his parenthetical phrase "though not uniquely." Our world is becoming more globalized by the second and, I suspect, more open to the possibility of conversion. American pop culture flows across international boundaries (for good or for ill) through the boundary-crashing flow of the internet, social media, and Twitter feeds. Openness to changing one's religion can't seem all that far-fetched in a day when people consider changing their gender! We may be experiencing the beginning rumblings of a worldwide revival that will prompt future historians to write books with titles like *The Event of the Twenty-First Century.*

A Personal Example

Spending hours of interviewing recent converts prompted me to reexamine my own journey to faith. Over time, we reinterpret our experiences through greater understanding of Scripture and deeper gratitude for the ways God worked in our life. We recall certain events we left out of earlier versions of our testimony. Seemingly insignificant happenstances now appear divinely ordained and pivotal. In a book filled with people's stories of faith, it seems only fair for me to tell you mine.

When I usually tell my story, I begin almost fifty years ago with Yom Kippur, the Jewish holiday of the Day of Atonement, when I was fifteen years old. Having grown up in a relatively secular Jewish home in a predominantly Gentile community, I learned, more than anything, that we were not like "them." We were Jews, and the one thing Jewish people knew for certain is that we didn't believe in Jesus. We also believed we are God's "chosen people" (although we rarely investigated exactly what that meant).

I found myself bothered by the disparity between my own lack of connection with God (despite my best efforts to obey his commandments) and the close connection some Gentile Christian friends seemed to have with "my God." I prayed in Hebrew, God's ordained dialect, but felt like my prayers went nowhere. They prayed in English—and sounded like they really connected.

So on that Yom Kippur, two years after my Bar Mitzvah (the milestone that I thought was supposed to bring me into a personal relationship with God), I decided to get this year's rendition of that holy day "right." I would spend all day in the synagogue and pray all the prayers prescribed for that day. I would confess all the sins included in the liturgy. And I would deny myself (see Lev. 16:29) many things—food, the luxury of driving in a car, and so forth—to fulfill my need for atonement. But it didn't work. I found myself walking home at sunset feeling no closer to God than I had felt twenty-four hours before.

And then I saw my shoes. I had gotten dressed up for the holiest day of the year in a nice suit and neatly polished dress shoes. But suddenly I remembered an important lesson from my Hebrew school education years before. On Yom Kippur, the rabbis taught that you're not allowed to wear leather shoes. They're too much of a luxury for a day of self-denial. That's why God still seemed distant to me. I had worn the wrong shoes! The discouragement was palpable.

But then I thought, "That's the stupidest thing in the world. That's how you get to know God? Obey this rule, obey that rule, wear the right shoes?" I do not remember praying but it must have had the same effect as a prayer when I muttered, "There's got to be another way." I now look back at that moment and see that God began to answer that prayer-like request in unexpected ways.

Shortly after that walk home in fine leather shoes, a friend invited me to his church's youth group. He wasn't particularly religious as far as I could tell, and his invitation appealed to other motives than spiritual longing. "It's a lot of fun and the girls are cute," he told me. So I went. And he was right!

For the next year, I attended almost every activity the youth group sponsored—roller skating parties, concerts, game nights, trips to the beach, you name it. Along the way, I heard the gospel. They always included some kind of "religious" component to every event. We'd sing songs and listen to a short sermon everywhere we went. Somehow, all that talk about Jesus didn't bother me too much. In fact, it intrigued me. Of course, whenever anyone asked what I thought about Jesus, I repeated what my parents, the entire Jewish community, and my rabbi trained me to say. "Oh, we don't believe in Jesus. We're Jewish. Jesus was just a good teacher. That's all."

Over time, people at that youth group (people my own age and their parents) started challenging me on that "Jesus was just a good teacher" line. More profoundly, I sensed that these people really did know God. They said they had "a personal relationship with God," and I believed them. And, as I think back about it now, I think I got jealous, just as Romans 11:11 says Jewish people will do when Gentiles know their God better than they do.

On one occasion, we took the church's minibus to the beach. As we pulled out of the parking lot, someone stood up at the front of the bus and said, "Hey, everyone! Let's pray." He closed his eyes and prayed, "Thank you, Lord, for this beautiful day and the chance we have to go to the beach. Please help us to have a good time, to stay safe, and to not get badly sunburned. In Jesus's name, Amen."

How odd, I thought. You don't pray on a bus on the way to a beach. I thought these people were lunatics. You don't bother the Almighty with things like sunburn! But that started me wondering. Maybe you do! Wouldn't it be great if you could know God that way and talk to him about anything? In English! As I interacted with those friends at the youth group, they repeatedly urged me to read the New Testament and another book called *Mere Christianity* by some guy named C. S. Lewis. They even gave me a paperback copy of the New Testament. But I had been warned not to read that book because of its anti-Semitism. My rabbi repeated many times that the New Testament was responsible for the Holocaust and other atrocities against our people. So I didn't read the book and forgot about that Lewis guy.

I went off to college a short time later and majored in beer. Well, the transcript said I majored in music, but a casual evaluation of how I spent my time during my freshman year would find more support of a fascination with Heineken than Haydn. I added some intellectual ingredients to that year of reading existentialist writers like Camus and Sartre and sprinkled in regular doses of Woody Allen movies and Kurt Vonnegut novels. If life is absurd, I thought, we might as well laugh about it.

My most serious efforts to find meaning or something transcendent to latch on to came every Saturday night when I attended concerts of the Philadelphia Orchestra. Music, I thought, was the one thing in life that was not absurd and had the greatest potential to satisfy. I kept hoping to find *the* piece of music that would propel me into the realm of satisfaction, a moment that would sate my spiritual hunger. But it never happened. Dvořák's symphonies came the closest for me. But every piece by every composer disappointed, if for no reason other than that it came to an end and the concert was over.

My sophomore year picked up at the same taverns and concerts where my freshman year left off. But on the night before the second semester of that year, a friend of mine died in a tragic accident that left me desperately wondering if life had any meaning at all. I sat at my friend's funeral and achingly realized I needed answers that Camus, Woody, Kurt, Dvořák, and Heineken couldn't provide.

I began to read the New Testament—the very paperback version my friends back at home had given me. (Up until that moment, I had not even cracked the front cover, but I *did* bring the book from home to my college dorm room—every semester!) And I went to the university library and took out *Mere Christianity* and read it in private places where no one could see me doing so. The gospel according to Matthew convinced me intellectually that Jesus was the Messiah (not just a mere rabbi). Lewis convinced me that Jesus was the one I was looking for.

What pulled it all together for me was Lewis's chapter on hope, where he discussed the many disappointments we experience in this life. We could try to overcome them by seeking other experiences that finally satisfy, or we could give up and become hopeless cynics. But Lewis articulated a third way to handle life's disappointments, the way of hope. In ways I continue to find delightful, I read Lewis's statement, "If I find in myself a desire which no experience in this world can satisfy, the most probable explanation is that I was made for another world."[20]

Now, here's a piece of my conversion puzzle I have only recently come to remember. Do you recall the guy I mentioned in chapter 2, the one who handed me a Christian magazine when I pumped gas into his car? At the time, that event may have seemed inconsequential. Now, I wonder if it may have been the most crucial. I took that magazine inside the gas station and, for hours, read every word. I believe it was on that day that I understood the logic of the gospel, the need for atonement, the incomplete nature of the law, and the call for an individual response of repentance and faith. I did not become a Christian until several years later, after reading Matthew and Lewis. But on that day at the gas station, my intellectual wrestling through some unknown person's Jesus magazine played a key role in my conversion.

> God assures us in his Word that "the prayer of a righteous person is powerful and effective" (James 5:16).

Did that gas customer pray for me after giving me the magazine? I don't know. It's quite likely that the kind of Christian who traveled around with gospel literature to distribute also prayed for God to use his efforts in eternally significant ways. Did the Christians at that church youth group pray for my salvation? I've since reconnected with some of them who have assured me that they most certainly did. Did intercessory prayer pave the way for repentant faith? God assures us in his Word that "the prayer of a righteous person is powerful and effective" (James 5:16).

I return to a question I have raised before. Is anyone really an "unlikely convert"? Was I? In one sense, we are all impossible converts—lost people, "dead in [our] transgressions and sins" (Eph. 2:1). But in another sense, no one's conversion is unlikely. Jesus's answer to his astonished disciples' question, "Who then can be saved?" was, "With man this is impossible, but with God all things are possible" (Matt. 19:25–26).

Let us, then, "devote [ourselves] to prayer, being watchful and thankful" (Col. 4:2). Who knows what God will do? Who can predict what we will see? And who can imagine how thankful we'll be for all eternity!

BRAINSTORMS: PRAYING FOR PEOPLE

It's good to have a list of nonbelievers you're praying for. It's a joy to move them from the list of "praying for salvation" to the list of "praying for spiritual growth." In the meantime, here are some ways to ask God for more than just, "Lord, save them!"

- Father in heaven, please open the eyes of my friend. Help her see what she cannot see yet. Help her understand things she can't seem to grasp. Remove the blinders so she can embrace you.
- Lord of the harvest, please make my friend dissatisfied with his life as it is right now. Give him a profound sense of unrest because he has not found his rest in you. Drive him to his knees as he sees the emptiness of life without you.
- Lord Jesus, may the reality of your death on the cross break through to my friend. Help her to receive what you've done as payment for sin. May the cross no longer be a stumbling block for her. Soften her heart.

- Oh Lord, my Shepherd, I'm weary of praying for my relative. It seems like nothing is happening—except that he's getting older. Help me to persevere in prayer. Remind me of how patient you've been with me and how tireless people were when they prayed for me.
- Almighty God, nothing is too difficult for you. My friend seems so angry and hardened against you. I really don't know what to say or how to get through to her. But that's not an obstacle for you. Please grant me wisdom in what to say and do, and grant her faith to receive your salvation.

EPILOGUE

I began this book with the account of Lawrence and the pigs. Let me tell you some more of his story. I first met Lawrence during his senior year in college. I had lunch with him again five years later after he had graduated and landed a great job.

What stood out during our first conversation was the question behind the question. Lawrence's apparent hang-up was about pigs. "Why did Jesus kill all those pigs by casting demons into them?" he wondered. But that wasn't the real issue. Rather, his underlying question was, "Is Christianity a stupid religion where people can't ask questions?" If so, he wanted no part of it. But when his Bible study leader offered a thoughtful answer, Lawrence concluded that his previous exposure to the Christian faith, where he was told to stop asking questions, wasn't the best. He now sensed that it was OK to ask questions and express doubt and wrestle with intellectual quandaries. God can handle our questions and meet us in our doubt.

> ## We need to listen for the question behind the question.

I concluded that we need to listen for the question behind the question. Often, there's a deeper, more substantive issue that may be the real hang-up for our non-Christian friends. Five years later, I discovered even deeper layers to Lawrence's story. He had grown in his faith and matured in beautiful ways. He joined a great church with a solid discipleship ministry and was part of a tight-knit community

171

group. When I reminded Lawrence about the pigs, he smiled. Then he told me something I never expected.

"You know, I've thought a lot about that Bible study when I asked that guy about the pigs. I think it's only been in the last year or so that I came to realize something else that was going on. I had no idea about it when you and I first talked. There was a reason I was drawn to that story about the guy who was delivered from all those demons." He paused, as if to search for the best words to say next. "It's because I was that guy."

He looked at me intently to see if I understood him. My puzzled face asked for more details. "That guy was in chains and was cutting himself and was a mess. Well, I was also in chains. I was doing horrible stuff to myself that was even worse than cutting myself. I was in the same kind of mess as that guy with all those demons in him. That's why I resonated with that story. It wasn't just about the pigs."

He recounted enough details for me to see he wasn't exaggerating. He repeated several times, "I didn't have to be told I was a sinner." Before moving away to college, he grew up in violent neighborhoods, got into fights on buses and at school, and saw a lot of difficult things. Being a pretty big guy, he learned how to defend himself and protect his single mother.

As he hesitantly told me things about his past, he zoomed in on how, before becoming a Christian, his episodes of violence never bothered him. Fighting seemed normal. After becoming a Christian, he marveled at how that changed. He now revisited moments from his past and realized, for the very first time, how awful his actions were. As he told me all this, his face changed from unexpressive to beaming. "It's amazing how God has forgiven me of all that."

We need to do more than just listen for the question behind the question. We should ask God to show us the drama behind the question. People may ask questions with cool, unexpressive faces. But behind those faces, dramas play out that we can't even imagine. They may ask about evil and suffering because they've become ensnared in evil and suffering. They may sit silently in a Bible study, but inside their heads the turmoil screams loudly. They may wander "randomly" into a worship service because their hearts are wandering desperately.

My hope is that this book will encourage you to reach out with the gospel to those around you—no matter how lost or far away they may seem. To us, they may look like unlikely converts. But to God, terms like *unlikely*, *difficult*, or *impossible* simply do not apply. May he use us to connect people's stories to the greatest story—the one we'll retell, delight in, and enjoy forever.

NOTES

Prologue

1. Walter Isaacson, *Benjamin Franklin: An American Life* (New York: Simon & Schuster, 2004), 312.
2. Max Planck, *Scientific Autobiography and Other Papers*, trans. F. Gaynor (1949; repr., New York: Philosophical Library, 2007), 33–34.
3. Jonathan Rauch, "Let It Be," *Atlantic*, May 2003, https://www .theatlantic.com/magazine/archive/2003/05/let-it-be/302726/.
4. Francis A. Schaeffer, *The Complete Works of Francis A. Schaeffer* (Wheaton, IL: Crossway, 1982), 149.
5. Russell Moore, "Are We Exiles?," July 24, 2015, RussellMoore .com, http://www.russellmoore.com/2015/07/14/are-we-exiles/. See also his extensive guide for living in a post-Christian world: *Onward: Engaging the Culture Without Losing the Gospel* (Nashville: B&H, 2015).
6. Timothy Keller, *Making Sense of God: An Invitation to the Skeptical* (New York: Viking, 2016), 4.
7. C. S. Lewis, *Mere Christianity* (New York: Touchstone, 1980), 21.
8. Lewis, *Mere Christianity*, 21.
9. Lewis, *Mere Christianity*, 36.
10. Lewis, *Mere Christianity*, 38.
11. C. S. Lewis, quoted in Justin Phillips, *C. S. Lewis in a Time of War* (San Francisco: HarperCollins, 2002), 82.
12. Wayne Grudem, *Systematic Theology: An Introduction to Biblical Doctrine* (Grand Rapids: Zondervan, 1994), 709.
13. C. S. Lewis, *Reflections on the Psalms* (1958; repr., New York: Harcourt, 1986), 1–2.

Chapter 1: Gradually

1. Don Everts and Doug Schaupp, *I Once Was Lost: What Post-modern Skeptics Taught Us About Their Path to Jesus* (Downers Grove, IL: InterVarsity, 2008), 23–24.

2. I've written more about this in *Bringing the Gospel Home: Witnessing to Family Members, Close Friends, and Others Who Know You Well* (Wheaton, IL: Crossway, 2011), 168–72. I readily admit that people are far more complex than what a single alphabetical label can convey. But many people have told me that the A to Z paradigm helps them consider a wide range of things to say to people at different stages of unbelief.

3. Adam Gopnik, introduction to *The Good Book: Writers Reflect on Favorite Bible Passages,* ed. Andrew Blauner (New York: Simon & Schuster, 2015), x.

4. See David G. Peterson, *The Acts of the Apostles* (Grand Rapids: Eerdmans, 2009), 487.

5. G. K. Chesterton, *The Everlasting Man* (1925; repr., San Francisco: Ignatius, 2008), 7.

6. For example, watch SpreadTruth.com's excellent video resource, *The Story,* video, 5:55, accessed March 27, 2019, https://thestoryfilm.com/watch/en.

7. Matt Chandler, *The Explicit Gospel* (Wheaton, IL: Crossway, 2014), 17.

8. I am indebted to Tim Keller for what I adapt as "routes of pre-evangelism." To explore these ideas in more depth, see chapter 5 of his *Preaching: Communicating Faith in an Age of Skepticism* (New York: Viking, 2015) and throughout his *Making Sense of God: An Invitation to the Skeptical* (New York: Viking, 2016).

9. C. S. Lewis, *Mere Christianity* (New York: Touchstone, 1980), 119–22. This idea did not originate with me. I'm paraphrasing my understanding, without apology but with reverent attribution, of the "Hope" chapter.

10. Lewis, *Mere Christianity,* 36.

Chapter 2: Communally

1. C. S. Lewis, "Membership" in *The Weight of Glory and Other Addresses*, rev. ed. (New York: HarperCollins, 1980), 163–64.

Chapter 3: Variously

1. Clifford Williams, *Existential Reasons for Belief in God: A Defense of Desires and Emotions for Faith* (Downers Grove, IL: InterVarsity, 2011), 17.
2. Williams, *Existential Reasons*, 14.
3. These are my adaptations of Williams's points. The wording in these quotes are mine, not his.
4. J. I. Packer and Mark Dever, *In My Place Condemned He Stood* (Wheaton, IL: Crossway, 2007), 21. Note especially Dever's concern that challenges to the centrality of substitutionary atonement continue to this day—even by some who call themselves evangelical (102).
5. To explore these terms more fully, I highly recommend Leon Morris, *The Atonement: Its Meaning and Significance* (Downers Grove, IL: InterVarsity, 1983); and John Stott, *The Cross of Christ* (Downers Grove, IL: InterVarsity, 1986).
6. I encourage reading and reflecting on these ideas with the help of Edward T. Welch, *Shame Interrupted: How God Lifts the Pain of Worthlessness and Rejection* (Greensboro, NC: New Growth, 2012), especially on page 186.
7. D. A. Carson, "Motivations to Appeal to in Our Hearers When We Preach for Conversion," *Themelios* 35, no. 2 (July 2010): 258–64. See especially his suggestions for evidence of these in numerous places in the New Testament.
8. Carson, "Motivations," 262.
9. Michael Ward, "Escape to Wallaby Wood," in *C. S. Lewis, Light-Bearer in the Shadowlands: The Evangelistic Vision of C. S. Lewis*, ed. Angus Menuge (Wheaton, IL: Crossway, 1997), 151.
10. *Merriam-Webster*, s.v. "capacious (*adj.*)," accessed March 27, 2019, https://www.merriam-webster.com/dictionary/capacious.

11. Alister McGrath, *Mere Apologetics: How to Help Seekers and Skeptics Find Faith* (Grand Rapids: Baker, 2012), 46.

12. McGrath, *Mere Apologetics*, 72.

13. Lloyd G. Carr, "Shalom," in *Theological Wordbook of the Old Testament*, vol. 2, ed. Robert Harris, Gleason Archer, and Bruce Waltke (Chicago: Moody, 1980), 930.

14. Carr, "Shalom," 931.

15. Williams, *Existential Reasons*, 12.

16. Owen Barfield, quoted in Philip Zaleski and Carol Zaleski, *The Fellowship: The Literary Lives of the Inklings: J. R. R. Tolkien, C. S. Lewis, Owen Barfield, Charles Williams* (New York: Farrar, Strauss and Giroux, 2015), 12.

17. Christopher Hitchens, *Mortality* (New York: Twelve, 2014), 41.

18. Christopher Hitchens, "Christopher Hitchens' Unusual and Radical Life," interview by Scott Simon, *Weekend Edition Saturday*, National Public Radio, June 5, 2010, https://www.npr.org/templates/story/story.php?storyId=127495653.

19. *Comedians in Cars Getting Coffee*, season 1, episode 10, "It's Bubbly Time, Jerry," produced by Jerry Seinfeld, featuring Michael Richards, aired September 27, 2012, on Crackle, https://vimeo.com/54271615.

20. Russell Moore, "The Sexual Revolution's Coming Refugee Crisis," RussellMoore.com, July 7, 2015, https://www.russellmoore.com/2015/07/07/the-sexual-revolutions-coming-refugee-crisis/.

21. Donna Freitas, *The End of Sex: How the Hookup Culture Is Leaving a Generation Unhappy, Sexually Unfulfilled, and Confused About Intimacy* (Philadelphia: Basic Books, 2013).

22. Freitas, *End of Sex*, 1.

23. Freitas, *End of Sex*, 9. Emphasis in original.

24. Mary Eberstadt, "The New Intolerance: An Adaptation of the Annual First Things Lecture," *First Things*, March 2015, https://www.firstthings.com/article/2015/03/the-new-intolerance.

25. Tim Keller, "The Gospel in All Its Forms," Gospel Coalition,

May 23, 2008, http://resources.thegospelcoalition.org/library /the-gospel-in-all-its-forms.

26. I discuss this verse's applicability to the specific "casting off of restraint" of homosexuality in *Questioning Evangelism* (Grand Rapids: Kregel, 2017), 158. I cannot address that issue much in this book. But all Christians would do well to acquaint themselves with the many helpful resources available today from authors such as Joe Dallas, Ed Shaw, Sam Allberry, Jeanette Howard, and others.

27. Francis Schaeffer, *He Is There and He Is Not Silent* (Carol Stream, IL: Tyndale, 1972).

Chapter 4: Supernaturally

1. J. I. Packer, *Evangelism and the Sovereignty of God* (Downers Grove, IL: InterVarsity, 1961), 106.

2. Charles Taylor, *A Secular Age* (Cambridge: Belknap Press, 2007), 3.

3. Robert D. Putnam and David E. Campbell, *American Grace: How Religion Divides and Unites Us* (New York: Simon & Schuster, 2010), 80.

4. Putnam and Campbell, *American Grace*, 80–82.

5. Putnam and Campbell, *American Grace*, 6.

6. "Religious Landscape Study," Pew Research Center, 2014, http://www.pewforum.org/religious-landscape-study/.

7. Tim Keller, "Public Faith: How to Share the Hope You Have in Christ," Gospel Coalition, January 29, 2018, https://www.thegospelcoalition.org/article/public-faith-share-hope-christ/.

8. Walter Kaiser has provided a very encouraging recounting of the many revivals in Scripture in his book *Revive Us Again: Biblical Principles for Revival Today* (Fearn, Ross-shire, UK: Christian Focus, 2013).

9. C. S. Lewis, *Yours, Jack: Spiritual Direction from C. S. Lewis* (New York: HarperCollins, 2008), 2–3.

Segue: The Power of Story

1. Much of the material in this section first appeared in Randy Newman, "Don't Just Share Your Testimony," Gospel Coalition, November 14, 2012, https://www.thegospelcoalition.org /article/dont-just-share-your-testimony/. The author retains the rights to this article.

Chapter 5: Carefully

1. Douglas J. Moo, *Galatians*, Baker Exegetical Commentary on the New Testament (Grand Rapids: Baker Academic, 2013), 181.
2. For a helpful discussion of the various ways the Scriptures discuss the love of God, see D. A. Carson, *The Difficult Doctrine of the Love of God* (Wheaton, IL: Crossway, 2000).
3. Some of this material first appeared in my article "Amazing Graces: How Complex the Sound," *Knowing and Doing*, C. S. Lewis Institute, February 26, 2018, http://www.cslewis institute.org/Amazing_Graces_How_Complex_the_Sound _FullArticle. Used with permission.
4. See 1 John 2:3, 5, 20, 29; 3:2, 10, 14, 16, 19, 24; 4:13, 16; 5:2, 18, 19, 20.
5. Leslie Newbigin, *Proper Confidence: Faith, Doubt, and Certainty in Christian Discipleship* (Grand Rapids: Eerdmans, 1995).
6. Many good resources on this topic exist. One of my favorites is Gregory E. Ganssle, *Thinking About God: First Steps in Philosophy* (Downers Grove, IL: InterVarsity, 2004).
7. "The Hitchens Transcript," *Portland Monthly*, December 17, 2009, https://www.pdxmonthly.com/articles/2009/12/17/chris topher-hitchens.
8. H. Richard Niebuhr, *The Kingdom of God in America* (Middletown, CT: Wesleyan, 1988), 193.

Chapter 6: Fearfully

1. See "The Story," video, 5:55, accessed March 27, 2019, https:// thestoryfilm.com/watch/en, and the many other resources at https://spreadtruth.com.

2. William Martin, *A Prophet with Honor: The Billy Graham Story* (New York: Quill, Morrow, 1991), 230.

3. Martin, *Prophet with Honor*, 236.

4. Martin, *Prophet with Honor*, 225.

5. Martin, *Prophet with Honor*, 228.

6. Martin, *Prophet with Honor*, 231.

7. Martin, *Prophet with Honor*, 235.

8. Rico Tice, *Honest Evangelism: How to Talk About Jesus Even When It's Tough* (Purcellville, VA: Good Book, 2015), 18.

9. "When Americans Say They Believe in God, What Do They Mean?," Pew Research Center, April 25, 2018, http://www.pew forum.org/2018/04/25/when-americans-say-they-believe-in -god-what-do-they-mean/.

10. This list is directly quoted from Christian Smith, *Soul Searching: The Religious and Spiritual Lives of American Teenagers* (New York: Oxford University Press, 2005), 162–63.

11. Smith, *Soul Searching*, 163.

12. Douglas Moo, *The Epistle to the Romans*, The New International Commentary on the New Testament (Grand Rapids: Eerdmans, 1996), 65.

13. You can find Thomas Chalmers's magnificent sermon "The Expulsive Power of a New Affection" online at several sources. For example, Monergism.com, accessed March 27, 2019, https://www.monergism.com/thethreshold/sdg/Chalmers,%20 Thomas%20-%20The%20Exlpulsive%20Power%20of%20 a%20New%20Af.pdf.

Chapter 7: Kindly

1. Deborah Tannen, *That's Not What I Meant! How Conversational Style Makes or Breaks Relationships* (New York: HarperCollins, 1986), 19.

2. See Theodore Zeldin, *Conversation: How Talk Can Change Our Lives* (Mahwah, NJ: HiddenSpring, 2000), 4.

3. Sherry Turkle, *Reclaiming Conversation: The Power of Talk in a Digital Age* (New York: Penguin, 2015), 3.

4. Kelly James Clark, "Reformed Epistemology Apologetics," in *Five Views on Apologetics*, ed. Stanley N. Gundry and Steven B. Cowan (Grand Rapids: Zondervan, 2000), 272.

5. Gary McIntosh, "Ask an Expert: How Are People Actually Coming to Faith Today?," *Biola Magazine* (Fall 2016): 18. See also Gary L. McIntosh, *Growing God's Church: How People Are Actually Coming to Faith Today* (Grand Rapids: Baker, 2016), 105–110.

6. To explore this important topic in more detail than I can address in this book, see Larry W. Hurtado, *Why on Earth Did Anyone Become a Christian in the First Centuries?* (Milwaukee, WI: Marquette University Press, 2016); Michael J. Kruger, *Christianity at the Crossroads* (Downers Grove, IL: InterVarsity Press, 2018); and Rodney Stark, *The Rise of Christianity* (Princeton, NJ: Princeton University Press, 1996).

7. Hurtado, *Christian in the First Centuries*, 126.

8. George Saunders, *Congratulations, by the Way: Some Thoughts on Kindness* (New York: Random House, 2014). All quotes of Saunders are from this book, which has no page numbers.

9. J. Alec Motyer, *The Prophecy of Isaiah: An Introduction and Commentary* (Downers Grove, IL: InterVarsity, 1999), 344.

10. For some reason the New International Version and English Standard Version render this first word of the verse, an emotional Hebrew exclamation, as "come." To be sure, "come" is repeated three more times in just one verse (Isa. 55:1). But the first word is more of an emotional plea: "Oh! All you who are thirsty, don't you see how good it would be if you would come?" See Motyer, *Prophecy of Isaiah*, 343.

Chapter 8: Prayerfully

1. D. A. Carson, *A Call to Spiritual Reformation: Priorities from Paul and His Prayers* (Grand Rapids: Baker, 1992), 147.

2. D. A. Carson, *Divine Sovereignty and Human Responsibility: Biblical Perspective in Tension* (Eugene, OR: Wipf & Stock, 2002). A more recent version of this book is available

as *Praying with Paul: A Call to Spiritual Reformation* (Grand Rapids: Baker, 2015).

3. Carson, *Divine Sovereignty*, 147.

4. A. T. Pierson, quoted by J. Edwin Orr at The National Prayer Conference, Dallas, October 26–29, 1976, during his presentation, "The Role of Prayer in Spiritual Awakening." See "The Role of Prayer in Spiritual Awakening by J. Edwin Orr," YouTube video, 26:14, November 10, 2015, https://www.youtube.com/watch?v=FW9Bb5tkOO4.

5. Walter C. Kaiser Jr., *Revive Us Again: Biblical Principles for Revival Today* (Fearn, Ross-shire, UK: Christian Focus, 2003), 3.

6. Kaiser, *Revive Us Again*, 6.

7. Kaiser, *Revive Us Again*, 15.

8. Martyn Lloyd-Jones, *Revival* (Wheaton, IL: Crossway, 1987), 162.

9. Collin Hansen and John Woodbridge, *A God-Sized Vision: Revival Stories That Stretch and Stir* (Grand Rapids: Zondervan, 2010), 14.

10. J. Edwin Orr, *The Flaming Tongue: The Impact of 20th Century Revivals* (Chicago: Moody, 1973), vii.

11. Richard Lovelace, *Dynamics of Spiritual Life: An Evangelical Theology of Renewal* (Downers Grove, IL: InterVarsity, 1979), 16.

12. Kathryn Long, quoted in Hanson and Woodbridge, *God-Sized Vision*, 77.

13. The following details come from Hansen and Woodbridge, *God-Sized Vision*, 77–97.

14. Orr, *The Flaming Tongue*, 18–19.

15. Orr, *The Flaming Tongue*, 19.

16. Lincoln A. Mullen, *The Chance of Salvation: A History of Conversion in America* (Cambridge: Harvard University Press, 2017), 4.

17. Emma Green, "Convert Nation," *Atlantic*, August 12, 2017, https://www.theatlantic.com/politics/archive/2017/08/conversions-lincoln-mullen/536151/.

18. Mullen, *Chance of Salvation*, 4.
19. Mullen, *Chance of Salvation*, 5.
20. C. S. Lewis, *Mere Christianity*, rev. ed. (San Francisco: Harper San Francisco, 2009), 136–37.

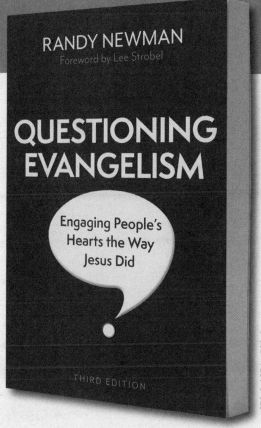

The Evangelism Study Bible

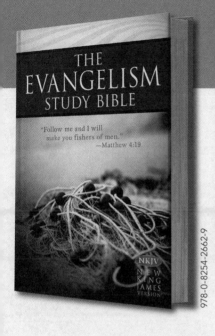

978-0-8254-2662-9

978-0-8254-2663-6

Four decades of Evantel's experience in training believers to share the good news in a clear and simple fashion has been paired with the one essential tool for evangelism: God's Word.

Inside you'll find:
- a brief, informative introduction to each Bible book, focusing on its contribution to evangelism
- more than 2,600 study notes pertaining to evangelism
- over 260 tips on practical issues in evangelism
- 125 in-depth articles on crucial issues
- 85 how-to features that provide hands-on advice
- 45 inspirational devotions
- easy-to-follow double-column format with explanatory notes
- helpful cross references
- biblical concordance
- full-color maps

KREGEL
PUBLICATIONS